THE GOLDEN STANDARD

Carving a path of excellence in a culture of complacency

Isaiah Satterthwaite

Contents

Acknowledgements

Thank you, God, for all that you are doing in my life. I am forever grateful. I pray that whoever reads this book will draw closer to your Word and be blessed.

A special thank you to my friend Solomon Cullum who inspired me to write this book. I appreciate all of your contributions and your encouragement throughout the entire writing and publishing process. I miss the conversations that we had at LU, and I am looking forward to your convocation speech whenever it occurs.

Thank you to my wife and son for your support and encouragement. I love you both so much!

Thank you to my parents for all of your insight and the many many conversations through the years. You have raised me into the man that I am today, and I love you all with all of my heart.

Thank you to Pastor Ralph, Pastor Hilton, and Pastor Marcellus for your wisdom and for your wonderful teaching at Ahavat. You all have challenged me in my walk with Yeshua and have really taken time out of your busy schedules to create a relationship with me.

Thank you, cousin TJ and cousin Trina for giving writing advice and for all of your support!

A special shout-out to my siblings, you guys are awesome!

Thank you to my great-grandparents, grandparents, aunts and uncles, cousins, co-workers, and friends. I am so blessed to be a part of your lives.

As my mom affectionately says, "I love my family!"

Introduction

Solomon Cullum is a Liberty alumnus who works in Congress with plans to eventually run for public office, with the end goal of becoming president of the United States. He enjoys playing golf and watching baseball, is a connoisseur of restaurants, bagel shops, and cookouts, and is always down for a hearty debate. Most importantly, he enjoys conversing with friends and sparking action with his "no nonsense" demeanor.

Isaiah Satterthwaite is also a proud Liberty University alumnus who works as an administrative and technical specialist in finance, accounting, and auditing. He enjoys playing basketball and other sports, hanging out with friends, and planning party events, and is a casual board game and retro video game enthusiast. Solomon and Isaiah currently reside in the DMV area and want to encourage other young adults to live their best lives in a humane and fulfilling way.

Liberty University's mission statement is to "Train Champions for Christ," and they do an amazing job preparing students to excel in their fields of choice while at Liberty. Unfortunately, some Christians are confused as to what it means to be champions for Christ, not just in the workplace but also in their homes, their hobbies, and in their communities. This book seeks to answer some of those questions and provide real-life examples of what a successful life of a Christian looks like.

This book is based off of the many conversations we have had while at Liberty University. We met through a mutual friend in the Student Government Association (SGA) at LU, and we ended up bonding over our similar viewpoints on life. This book is also to help us be accountable so we can practice what we preach. One thing that we often talked about at Liberty was the herd culture that our society practices, in that a small majority of people can quickly start a wide movement that can sweep everyone else into. For example, before the COVID-19 quarantine started, Solomon would always be informing me about the hysteria that was on the rise and how a big change (and a potential power grab) was going to happen. Lo and behold, the virus changed everyone's lives (some permanently), and many people were swept into thinking that extreme measures were the only way to stop the spread. While there is still controversy on how COVID-19 should be dealt with today, most people now concede that some of the regulations were a bit excessive. From our conversations during the "2 weeks to stop the spread" that spanned over the entire 2020 year, we noticed that if it is that easy to shut down society in a once thought "unthinkable" way, how easy would it be to get people to do other things? From movements such as BLM and racism, MAGA culture, LGBT activism, climate control, world politics, and other random quarrels and disputes, there are so many things that can invigorate copious amounts of emotion and reactions. All of this is happening while Christianity is moving away from the forefront of our society and is being replaced with secularism, degeneracy, and a strange new wave of everyone being interested in political control, and in particular a large, united world order. Growing up, the American dream was one of three options:

1. **Start a family and get a cute house with a chill vacation twice a year.**

2. Create a successful business and or have a fulfilling career.

3. Travel and see the wonders of the world.

While those things are still desires that most people have, what those things intrinsically are is currently changing. There are different definitions of what a family or a fulfilling career is, and we often see polarization between two parts of society over these things. A factor in this is that many people no longer believe that certain dreams are even attainable anymore, especially because of the economy, climate, or other things that are seemingly out of their control. We are seeing a microwave mentality that is taking over western society and seeping into all aspects of life. Because it is harder to go on a fancy vacation or make money or raise a family, we see people turning to immediate gratification such as an overindulgence in drinking alcohol, drugs, promiscuous sexual activities and orientation, and even excessively participating in things that are not inherently bad such as music, video games, and movies. People can blame these things on capitalism making certain vices more accessible, but at the end of the day people's willpower has gone down.

Why is that the case? Some people don't care enough to put in the effort, some don't realize that they are being controlled by mindless consumerism, and some don't fully understand the benefits that one gets when one becomes disciplined. While we see the effects that laziness and complacency have on our outward behaviors, how we react to the world is not based on our brain and rational thinking but on how our mind and soul operate. (An example of this is we know rationally that it is good to get 8 hours of rest so we can be wide awake for work in the morning, but sometimes our inward desires of wanting to stay up late and watch a feel-good movie overpower our rational logic of getting the necessary hours of rest.)

Pop culture promoting the ideals of "follow your heart" and "do what you want" has really inspired people to follow their inward desires in unhealthy manners. Pairing that feeling of freedom with the feeling of entitlement leads to short term gratification, but it eventually becomes a problem, especially because people aren't always free to do what they desire to the fullest extent, and people are not entitled to everything that they think they are. When people forcibly follow their desires, even when it is not beneficial to do so, in the end it slowly becomes a death spiral toward unhappiness and resentment. For example, some people feel like they deserve to have a significant amount of money without having to do a significant amount of work (Entitlement) so that they can spend their time purchasing and playing more MMO RPGs (Freedom). After receiving a couple thousand from parents and grandparents to pay their rent and food bills, things go smoothly for a few weeks as one can play as much as he would like with minimal downtime. But when next month rolls around, the person wakes up to a nearly empty bank account and rent coming right around the corner, forcing the person to either have to work to be able to cover his expenses, or to beg for more money. This is when it is no longer beneficial for a person to follow his sense of entitlement and freedom; it's time to get a job. But if the person continues to play video games all day and beg for money from relatives or the government, then he becomes a burden to society and less people will want to help him out as he is being more and more selfish. Socialist ideals are largely on the rise because people do not want to take individual responsibility. The phrase "you will own nothing and be happy" is really a true statement for a lot of people as people are sadly content with indulging themselves in superficial things such as Netflix, TikTok, and Gacha games.

Now, by no means am I saying that it is wrong to have freedom, and we as humans are entitled to life in a rudimentary perspective, but what I am saying is that there are parameters that must be followed within being able to do whatever one wants. We should have free will to live our lives however we want, but within reason of course. Freedom at its max level ends up being anarchy, and entitlement at its extreme leads to justification of anything.

From a spiritual perspective, human nature is inherently flawed, so if everyone were to live exactly how they wanted without regard for other people, pure chaos would ensue. So how do we apply the following quote from the Declaration of Independence?

> "We hold these truths to be self-evident, that all men are created equal, that they are endowed by their Creator with certain unalienable Rights, that among these are Life, Liberty and the pursuit of Happiness."
> – Thomas Jefferson

How do we pursue happiness while at the same time maintaining life and liberty? In modern culture, those things are no longer synonymous. People no longer want to pursue their lives in peace, but they want others to validate/affirm their pursuits as well. Some people also feel like other people's pursuits of happiness are in conflict with their own pursuits and feel like they need to champion their desires to protect their "rights." Most people understand that happiness can be subjective, but what does "life" constitute? What does it mean to have liberty?

Because this nation was founded upon Christian principles, we can rightfully say that the Declaration of Independence is not stating that people are justified in doing harmful things such as stealing or murdering others, even if it brings joy. There are parameters to freedom that are determined by the laws of the land, which in whole should be based on God's Word. Not all man-made laws are godly, but that is a separate topic for a separate book. We should follow the laws of the land and obey God's Word to live a truly respectable life, and we need to apply both of those ethics in all of our day-to-day activities to live an honorable and spiritually fulfilling life. (Assuming that the laws are aligned with God's Word, of course.)

This is why we have written this book: to guide others toward the path of righteousness and contentment and to hold ourselves accountable to the high standards that God has set for us and allows us to attain. Before we get into the Gold Standard, we want to preface some of our beliefs that will be implied in our book.

1. **God's Word is the ultimate truth.**

2. **Everything has some amount of truth to it, which is what makes lies so dangerous.**

3. **Everyone is at a different stage in their walk with God, so some of these opinions may not be as easy to apply for different believers in different stages in their walk.**

So, let's get into why God's Word is the ultimate truth.

Why We Believe

"FOR GOD SO LOVED THE WORLD THAT HE GAVE HIS ONLY BEGOTTEN SON, THAT WHOEVER BELIEVES IN HIM SHOULD NOT PERISH BUT HAVE EVERLASTING LIFE. FOR GOD DID NOT SEND HIS SON INTO THE WORLD TO CONDEMN THE WORLD, BUT THAT THE WORLD THROUGH HIM MIGHT BE SAVED." JOHN 3:16-17 (NKJV)

Being raised in a Christian home, we had the privilege of living in a stable environment and knowing the things of God from a very young age. Some people may say that we have been brainwashed, but we both came to truly believe in our own faith during our teenage years. There are many different beliefs that people have, and I think everyone at some point in time has to contemplate "What is my calling in life? Why do I exist?" There are different answers to these questions, ranging from "there is no true purpose in life" to "our lives are meant to progress the human race and be a net positive to society" to "religion gives us a calling."

I think that there must be more to this life, simply because of the concept of morality. People have a general sense that some things are better than other things (it is better to help an old lady across the street instead of kicking a puppy, for example), and there has to be a reason behind this morality. If morality is based on the society that we live in, then that would mean that right and wrong (and ultimately truth) is relative to the environment that one is in. (Maybe that is why major corporations that promote "social justice" turn a blind eye to misdeeds in other countries in hopes of keeping their businesses there). I think this viewpoint does not work in the long run, as that means that justice would also be relative. If there is no God, then Hitler would have lived a lavish lifestyle with no worries about eternal damnation. The fact that people can live their lives in pure evil and get away with it just doesn't sit right with me. Everyone has a conscience at some point in their lives and an internal sense of what is right and what is wrong, even if people try to deny or justify it (that is where guilt comes in). For example, atheists and believers alike generally agree that it is good to give money to a good charity and it is bad to steal candy from a baby, and they will associate good and bad emotions with each action.

Obviously, people know that it is wrong to steal, but sometimes people will do it because they either feel like they must in order to survive, because they want to experience the thrill of attempted robbery, because they want to make money quickly, or because they feel like there are not any serious consequences to getting caught. These are simple examples of people justifying wrong actions. The human brain can justify anything if it truly wants to (look at the horrible experiments done in human history in the name of "science") which is why I think it is impossible to trust our own minds to rationalize every single thing.

Other questions that can be rationalized in any manner are questions such as the following:

1. **What is the point of life?**

2. **What is a good life?**

3. **What makes some choices better than others?**

4. **And most importantly, why do we have consciousness that gives us an innate desire of good and bad?"**

Once again, the point of life can vary depending on whatever you want it to be, but that does cause a lot of issues. A good life for some people could be the life of a drug addict because even though they don't live for very long and have a bunch of medical challenges, they experience the powerful "highs" and sensations that normal people never really experience as often or as intensely. Obviously, most people will agree that abusing drugs is bad as they wreak havoc on your long-term health (don't do drugs; stay in school), but without an intrinsic reason to why life preservation is beneficial then all vices would be deemed acceptable as long as it makes you "happy," regardless of the detrimental effects in the future. As much as people may argue for these things, the majority of people in the world are very concerned about their long term survival and will avoid doing things that can cause a quick death (even if it means forgoing immediate pleasures). Why is that?

All these qualms of morality, truth, and justice lead back to religion, one way or another, and Christianity makes a strong case why it is the only true religion. While we won't get into a deep dive of Christian theology in this book, we believe in God, His Son Jesus, and the Holy Spirit because there is so much evidence of a Creator. We also believe because our faith in our Creator has given us an opportunity to turn away from our wicked ways, and God will bring true justice to those who follow righteousness and those who do not.

Let's take it back a little bit and walk through all of those points. The evidence of a Creator is shown through the world around us, the "creation." If something exists in the world, then something had to create it. In the same manner that a baby must have a father and mother to exist, someone had to have created the trees, the rocks, the water, and so forth. The world is way too detailed for it to not have a creator.

Since there is a Creator, there should be a reason why the creation was created. For example, an artist creates a painting to appreciate the beauty of a sunset, an engineer creates a robot to do a certain task (such as a robotic vacuum), and since we are created by something, what is our purpose? To live out our parents' hopes and dreams? To seize the day and party every night? Or are we created to honor our Creator through every aspect of our lives? The last sentence makes the most sense if using rational logic, but then another question arises: How do we honor God?

The Bible says in Genesis that God created mankind (Adam and Eve) in "His image" and wants us humans to be able to hang out with Him and appreciate and take care of the world that He gave us. We honor God by following His ways and being good stewards in the world. God also gave us free will to do whatever we want, and Adam and Eve chose to eat the fruit of "knowledge of good and evil" even though God told them not to. (Read the first couple of chapters in Genesis for a full reference of the story.) Because they disobeyed God and were now ashamed to be with Him, they had to leave His presence. Eventually sin became increasingly worse as the years went by. Fortunately for us, God had a master plan to redeem us all from our evil ways by sending His Son Jesus to pay the price for our sins and to transform our hearts to seek to follow God's ways and no longer follow the whims of our selfish desires.

Religions outside of Christianity have their arguments, but they don't have the same convincing evidence that Christianity does. For example, Buddhists think that morality, meditation, and knowledge are the means to enlightenment, and they frequently meditate because they think it promotes the awakening of truth. The principles of morality and meditation are noble pursuits, but the question remains: who decides morality? Buddhists do not believe in a theistic God, so it is a little bit confusing (from an outsider's perspective) what constitutes morality for them. That all being said, morality from a Christian perspective is based on the Ten Commandments with it all being summed up as loving the Lord your God with all your heart, soul, and strength and by loving your neighbor as yourself. It is impossible to do those things on our own merit, as no one has ever lived a perfect life. But, by accepting Jesus Christ and the Holy Spirit into your heart, God gives us the ability to resist temptation and be holy unto Him.

I also think that it is interesting how many similarities there are between Islam, Judaism, and Christianity (arguably the three most controversial religions) in terms of the Old Testament. They all believe that Abraham was the ancestor of Isaac and Ishmael, Jerusalem and Israel play a big role in all three religions, and the Bible, the Talmud, and the Quran all have parts that are similar. But there are some things that make Christianity better than Islam and Judaism. Islam has many similarities to Christianity, but there are some controversial things that make believing in Islam much more difficult than Christianity. Muhammad (Islam's main prophet) for example was certain that Jesus was not the Son of God, even though Jesus fulfilled all the prophecies of the prophets in the Old Testament. Muhammad also claimed to be the only one who received the Quran, and in contrast the Bible was written by dozens of people, and none of the writings in the Bible conflict with each other. The Quran also has some things that are a little bit problematic such as being okay with men marrying minors (like pre-pubescent minors) and the whole jihad movement. Muhammad also was not necessarily a righteous man if one wishes to look at some of the misdeeds that he did. The biggest reason why Islam is not the true religion is because there is no redeemer for one's sins. As stated earlier, it is impossible for everyone to live a holy life 24/7, and it is almost impossible for people to follow man-made rules, let alone follow God's Word. How can someone do the right thing 100% of the time without supernatural help? And because God is holy, there is not a smidge of sin that can be allowed in God's presence. Therefore, there needs to be a middleman (Jesus), someone who can take the punishment for our sins so we can be in God's presence.

In the Tanach, Judaism (in my opinion, Judaism is the closest religion to Christianity) shows us that God has created special rituals and practices for the Israeli people (such as keeping kosher, honoring the Sabbath, wearing four cornered garments, etc.) so that they can stand out from other nations and be set apart for God. When someone in the camp sinned, there would be various sacrifices and offerings made as an atonement so that God could still dwell with them in their encampment. Modern traditional Judaism believes that their Messiah has not come yet, and they are still waiting for His coming. Although Jews do not sacrifice animals anymore, they seek to be forgiven for their sins through prayer and acts of repentance. Once again, the problem is the lack of a middleman. Let's provide one last example (for now):

If a man commits a crime, then justice should be enacted. Let's say this dude vandalized a window. Justice would be that the man would either repair the window or pay for the damages, or if he was unable to pay, he would either work his debts off or go to jail. Now, let's say that the man was really sorry for his actions and promised the judge that he would not do it again. It would not be fair to the owner of the window if the judge said, "Gee, you do seem pretty remorseful for your actions, so I will let you go free, no strings attached." Someone has to pay the cost of repairing the window. This is the same problem of someone who is praying to God to forgive them of their sins if they do not believe in Jesus. It would be unjust for God to forgive that person because of the consequences that their sin had.

This is why Christianity is the only true religion; Jesus died on the cross for everyone's sins and became our mediator so that our sins became Jesus' sins. Jesus takes the blame and bears the price for our sins and allows us to be holy unto God. It's a miracle!

Now, Christian theology can get very dense, but the basis that anyone needs to know about Christianity is that God created mankind to hang out with Him, mankind rebelled by choosing to follow their own wicked ways, and God sent His Son to die for everyone's sins so that we can once again dwell with God. (John 3:16)

Now that we've explained why we believe in God's Word being the ultimate truth, we can go into the second point that we made earlier, which is that "Everything has some amount of truth to it, which is what makes lies so dangerous." As stated earlier, I think that all religions have some type of "merit" to them that makes them believable, otherwise no one would follow them. For example, many religions have a moral system, and there are good ethical things that come from those systems. Honoring your elders in and of itself is a wise thing to do and is a big principle that Hindus try to follow. Because it is good to show respect to others, does that mean that Hinduism is a true religion? No, it does not. Why? Because Hinduism teaches that through your deeds you can achieve a form of salvation, and as stated earlier, it is impossible to live a perfect life; no matter what you do, it will not be enough. You need a savior to help you. But people can get into Hinduism because they feel good that they are living an ethical life and that there is tangible evidence for the existence of karma (which it does to an extent). This is why we need to focus on all truthful things, not just taking one segment of truth. We can filter out truth from the lies based on what God's Word says. If it contradicts the Bible, it is probably bad.

Lies need to mimic the truth as much as possible so they can fool as many people as possible. An easy example of this is AI deep fakes, as they resemble a prominent figure in society and the AI emulates the person's speech and looks to have them say whatever the coder wants to say. In the beginning of AI technology, deep fakes looked nothing like the real person, but as time is progressing it is very hard to discern whether a speech or podcast on the internet was made by a human or by a chatbot. The devil has been using lies for all of eternity to confuse as many people as possible and get millions of people to believe in something other than Christianity, from perverting the culture and society and even people who claim to be Christian! From the Crusades, Nazis, different cults, and many other examples, people have totally misrepresented the word "Christian" to the point that some Christians don't even call themselves Christians because they do not want to associate themselves with that name. (Read the book *Identity Theft* by Ron Cantor for more information on the deconstruction of the Christian religion.) We as believers in God need to make sure that we are not misrepresenting God's kingdom.

How do we not misrepresent God's kingdom? By aligning ourselves as closely as we can to the Bible. God's Word gives us very clear blueprints on how we should live our lives. We have mentioned that the two greatest commandments are to love God with everything you have and to love your neighbor as yourself, and God goes into detail on countless subjects and elaborates His will in topics ranging from money, marriage, management of one's affairs, and everything in between. For reference, the book of Proverbs is one of the most practical books in the Bible for those who are looking to make wise choices in their lives, and the book of Psalms shows us how to sing praises to God. When people follow the wise principles that God has laid out, they automatically learn the truths of God and how those truths are beneficial to their lives. When people pervert the truths to come up with their own version of "wise" behavior, we see time and time again how that leads to trouble. The definition of a lie is a false statement. If it is not true, it is a lie, no matter how close it is to the truth. So, if we live our lives out with only part of God's Word (such as trying to do good deeds without accepting Jesus into one's heart) we are not living out the truth.

This brings us to our third point: "Everyone is at a different stage in their walk with God." For some people, it is easy to get along with others and do good deeds, but for others it can be a bit of a struggle. That also applies to believers in Christ as well. When someone truly accepts Jesus into their heart, the Holy Spirit of God also enters one's body and essentially helps to heighten one's sense of wisdom (and guilt) and point the person in the right direction. However, just because people have the Holy Spirit does not mean that they always heed it. Some people choose not to follow their moral compass, or they may not be aware of the full consequences of their actions. For others, the cycle of being tempted, committing a sin, feeling regret, and seeking repentance is sadly a very common issue. Temptation can be an intense force, or it can be like a soft whisper. The dangerous thing about temptation is that it can really distract your judgment and obscure the realities that the long-term effects of sin have. Fortunately for us, God promises us that we can overcome our fleshly desires in 1 Corinthians 10:13, which says the following:

> *"No temptation has overtaken you except such as is common to man; but God is faithful, who will not allow you to be tempted beyond what you are able, but with the temptation will also make the way of escape, that you may be able to bear it." (NKJV)*

If we draw close to God, God will help us resist against the will to sin, but we have to put our trust in God and forgo the "microwave mentality" that is consuming our generation.

Some try to justify committing a sin by saying that because Jesus died for our sins so it doesn't matter how we live as long as we believe that Jesus is our savior. The apostle Paul has a perfect response to this claim in Romans 6:1-2, which says the following:

> *"What shall we say then? Shall we continue in sin that grace may abound? Certainly not! How shall we who died to sin live any longer in it?"*

Although we are forgiven of our sins, we should not continue sinning, as we have been saved from that. Why would we want to sin over and over again if we already asked Jesus to save us from our sin? It is one thing to struggle with a sin and seek to eradicate any addictions, but it is no good if we are complacent in sinning every day.

The Gold Standard of living a righteous life in modern times is getting more and more difficult as we are beginning to live in a "Brave New World" in the sense that the lust of the eye, the lust of the flesh, and the pride of life are the most important things of this world, but we are called to a higher standard. Philippians 4:13 says that "we can do all things through Christ who gives us strength," and God has given us the ability to be the best person we can be without having to walk in sin. With that being said, let's get into the meat of our book.

The Gold Standard

"AND WHATEVER YOU DO, DO IT HEARTILY, AS TO THE LORD AND NOT TO MEN, KNOWING THAT FROM THE LORD YOU WILL RECEIVE THE REWARD OF THE INHERITANCE; FOR YOU SERVE THE LORD CHRIST." COLOSSIANS 3:23-24 (NKJV)

Simply put, if it is Christian then it ought to be better. Christians should not live their lives as losers, but as exceptional individuals that are striving to share a positive outlook to the world. Christians should strive to be among the very best in whatever vocation they are in and be a good witness to others. Christians should seek to excel in whatever position they are in, whether it being a worker at a fast-food company or at a million-dollar corporation. Of course, it is hard (some might even say impossible) to live life going 100% at everything you do, but it is a noble pursuit to perform above expectations in life. For example, Christians should be synonymous with people who are providing quality customer service because Christians should actually care about the people they are serving (Chick-fil-A is a big example). Christians should integrate as much as they reasonably can in society, and when society rejects us, we can survive on our own. 1 Thessalonians 4 is what we base the standard of living a good life; living humble and honorable lives unto God.

In February 2023, Isaiah gave a small message on a Torah portion called "Terumah" (meaning "offering") that covered Exodus 25 to Exodus 27:2. These chapters are basically God's outline for various contributions and offerings that the Israelites can give, and how the donations from the Israelites will be used to build a tabernacle of worship that is dedicated to God. We can apply these verses to show just how important it is to have standards and to know how to attain those standards.

So, the two main points that Isaiah took away from this Torah portion are the following:

1. **God has high standards for His people, and we need to follow those standards if we want to hang out with Him.**

2. **Because our body is a living temple, we should be careful what things we are building our temple out of (not just physically but also spiritually).**

From the first verses in Exodus 25, we see the high quality in the materials that God is requiring and how anything else outside of God's criteria will not be accepted. God only wants the best of the best, and He is very specific about it.

Now it's interesting to note that the Israelites had all of these valuables while in the middle of the desert. It was hot outside but the Israelites were just hauling all their gold and acacia wood and gemstones and stuff. I think that is very interesting...

If we go back to Exodus 12, we see how the Israelites were given various gifts from the Egyptians when they were freed from slavery, and they had been carrying those gifts with them all throughout their journey so far, and it's cool to see how those gifts came into play so that they could be used for God's glory.

I like to think that there were some people that were watching the Israelites pass through their side of town just wondering things like "bro, where'd you get all that money from?" or "why are they carrying so much unnecessary stuff?"

This Torah portion is a good reminder as well that it's not a bad thing to have gold and gems and other valuable resources, as long as we are honoring God with our possessions. And that applies whether you want to be a millionaire or minimalistic; there is nothing intrinsically wrong with nice things. So, we need to be careful when judging others on the things they have.

For example, In the Haftorah in 1 Kings 6, we see Solomon (the richest man alive) use his treasures and wisdom to design arguably the most beautiful (and one of the most expensive) temples in history, estimated to be worth millions and billions of dollars today (before inflation).

Now before we go and say, "good grief, that money should have been used to feed the poor," while reading it, we see God telling Solomon how exactly to build the temple.

1 Kings 6:12-13 in particular covers God commanding Solomon on how important it is to follow God's standards.

It's really cool to see in the Torah and the Haftorah how God is very clear in what the standards are for building the temple, down to every item and every measurement. It's also cool how when we apply God's standards to our lives exactly how God tells us to, we end up drawing close to God. And that's pretty cool, good vibes all around. The Bible tells us that the way that we live our lives should be very similar to the standards that were set in Torah. We are to be set apart so that outsiders will recognize the greatness of God. We read about this in 1 Corinthians 3:16-17 which says the following:

> *"Do you not know that you are the temple of God and that the Spirit of God dwells in you? If anyone defiles the temple of God, God will destroy him. For the temple of God is holy, which temple you are."*

Now I've been around a lot of people who talk about our physical bodies being a temple of God and how we should take care of ourselves by exercising, watching what we eat with various diets, and taking different measures to ensure that we live healthy lives.

That stuff is cool for sure, but I think that we should take that same energy (and more) and watch what we are intaking from a spiritual perspective, whether it's a movie, music, social media, videos games, even the thoughts that we have...I'm not saying we shouldn't enjoy different outlets of entertainment, but we should question whether those things as a whole are things listed in Philippians 4:8, which says to think on things that are true, noble, just, pure, lovely, and of good repute.

In the same manner of the phrase "you are what you eat," I think that can also be applied to our spiritual diet. If we are constantly subjecting ourselves to ungodly things, it's going to be pretty hard to give our lives as a daily sacrifice that is acceptable to God. If we live righteously, it will be easier for us to use our blessings and spiritual gifts to bring praises to God's name. Which is why praise, worship, prayer, and meditation in God's Word are so essential to our walk with God.

In summary, in the Torah portion you see God instructing the Israelites to gather the best of the best materials to build a Holy Temple of worship, and we see that God has called us to take the fruits of the spirit and use them as a basis to build our lives upon.

When we look at our modern day lives, we still know what God's standards are in our lives, and they can be summed up by the two greatest commandments (Love the Lord your God with all your heart, soul, and strength, and love your neighbor as yourself). Easy to say, sometimes hard to do.

With that being said, we challenge everyone to examine your life and see what things are pleasing to God and what things need to be left behind.

The Christian faith is the foundational bedrock from which all things come. Not only is Christianity the indisputable truth about our world but it is also a shining example of fundamental principles, beliefs, and behavior that should be exemplified daily. Christians across the world, but especially in the United States, should take great confidence in this, not only because we as believers know and understand the truth about God's Word and the world around us but also because we will be victorious in the end as Christ will return and deliver all of us from the sins and evil of the fallen world we live in. Having said that, we as Christians must consistently strive for excellence in every area of society.

Over the years, we have seen Christians begin to waver and deteriorate in the core belief of striving for excellence and achieving exceptionalism on all societal levels. During this time, we have seen our societal institutions begin to collapse, the Christian church weekend, the family unit deteriorating, our sports exemplifying non-Christian attitudes, and our governments becoming hostile and contradicting the founding principles of our nation, which is the Judeo-Christian faith. The Christian church and believers all across this country need to recognize that the absence of morals, personal responsibility, and a lack of ambitious Christians taking charge are the reasons why society continues to deteriorate in every facet of everyday life. It is essential that we establish the core fundamental belief of Christians, no matter what background you came from, your personal preferences, or your culture.

We must reassert ourselves on the biggest stages of our society. Having successful Christian athletes, prominent politicians, exceptional artists and musicians, and individuals in the entertainment news spheres ultimately allow for Christian and American exceptionalism to be projected on the national front and allow a revival to be made possible in our land. If it is Christian, it ought to be better; no mediocrity and no losing. Achieving excellence must be at the forefront of a new ambitious plan that Christians must establish to preserve our nation's founding and to reestablish the morality that has allowed our country to be so successful and prosperous over the years.

It should be the duty of every believer to use his or her platform and vocation to not only spread the word of God and evangelize to nonbelievers within their area of influence, but also to be ambitious champions for the faith and the principles that a Christian society should abide by. Complacency and apathy will not accomplish a positive and impactful trajectory. Instead, we should go into the world and spread the goodness and truths of the Bible through our behaviors, behaviors that are articulated through Scripture.

Over the last few years, we have seen the Christian church put a strong emphasis on communicating the grace of God. While this is definitely an important and crucial message and an attribute of Christ himself, we have begun to use the grace of God as an excuse to not be the best possible individuals we can be on every level. Just because of that we know that we are saved and will spend eternity with Christ and that God will eventually come down in decisive victory over evil, does not give us the opportunity to be lazy and go with the status quo until He arrives. And we are called to be in the world but not of it. Every opportunity in the workplace, the sports world, the media entertainment arena, and other important areas in our society should be used as a stage to project the truth of Christ. Christians being active, ambitious, and successful in various avenues throughout our culture is a subtle but effective strategy of preaching the Word of God to individuals that do not know Him. We always think of examples or stories of specific evangelism techniques of discussing Christ one-on-one with a non-believer, but we must comprehend that the actions we do every single day are just as effective in evangelizing to those who need to hear the truth and grace of God. When Christians perform their daily duties with success and humility and carry themselves in confidence, then those who do not believe wonder how this is possible and therefore want to know how it is done. This will ultimately give you as an individual a prime opportunity to share with unbelievers that it is because of God's grace, God's power, and His guidance that allows you to be able to live the life that you do and shapes the behaviors that you exemplify.

The gold standard is the foundation to not only the Christian faith but also how we should live our lives on an everyday basis. It's more than a mantra and more than a belief; it is a movement to establish a consistent behavior that correlates with exceptional behavior and performance. It doesn't matter how much money you make or how high one is on the food chain; God works through everyone equally. The Christian faith is emulated in one's actions. Whether one is working for the Waste Management systems, as an accountant in Vanguard, or as a congressman, the same principles apply. We should acknowledge the blessings that God has given us (spiritual, physical, and emotional), and we should go to our jobs and give everything that we have as gratitude for God.

People in higher positions in society must hold themselves to a higher standard as they are in the public eye. How much more surprising is it when people who are in lower paying jobs perform their jobs with exceptionalism? Working in lower paying jobs will allow people to show the gold standard and stand out to their peers, because their peers are looking for an avenue of contentment and fulfillment.

People who do an exceptional job at their duties while pleasantly pleasing people often have opportunities to elevate to higher positions sooner than the average rate, have a better outlook on their work environment, and create positive relationships with coworkers and customers.

Often raises are given based on performance and tenure. If you perform well, you will most likely be able to continue working at your job for longer than someone who is not doing as well as you. It is easier to work better if you have a positive outlook, which in turn also makes you more amenable to demands from your manager or requests from customers.

Let's provide a proverbial example of how one can set the standard as a blue-collar customer service Sodexo worker, and Isaiah will provide real scenarios of his lived experiences as sales associates.

For a Sodexo worker, it is grueling work providing quality customer service, receiving orders from desperate hungry customers, and maintaining a clean working environment, all while having a big smile on your face for eight full working hours.

Working in the food service industry may seem tedious; however, the ability to fellowship over food has been instrumental to the current day. It is highlighted in various parts of Scripture. Jesus made clear intentions to fellowship with His followers. How is a cook in Jesus' time making pita bread different from a cook in the present day flipping burgers? Having the proper mindset and behavior will allow the opportunity for others to fellowship with their friends.

The way food is prepared has a tremendous impact on the level of conversation, as we all have experienced a conversation shift based on the way food tastes, for better or for worse.

How you do your work has a trickle-down effect on other people's lives. No one knows the plans and opportunities that will come, but if one is always prepared, he will be able to share the goodness of God to whomever he encounters, and at the very least become a respectable cook. If you establish a good rapport and customers begin coming specifically for your food, eventually some people may want to get to know you and may even confide in you for advice when you have a break. When Solomon and Isaiah were on campus, there were certain chefs that gained a reputation of making exceptional meals and had great service, and students were able to get to know them on a more personal basis during breaks and outside of working hours. Isaiah even witnessed several students giving thoughtful parting gifts to a well-respected lead cook because of her kindness and mannerisms that she bestowed over the years that she worked there. She impacted other workers by inspiring them to always give their best and to meet the needs of the customer.

When Isaiah was a sales associate at a retail clothing store, he would work as much as he could (without burning himself out) and keep the store in tip top shape, doing his best to get to know customers so he could serve their needs. Because Isaiah was representing his school, his family, and ultimately God to his coworkers, who may or may not have had the same convictions that he held, he wanted to do his best to quickly learn tasks such as the complex folding techniques that could be quite perplexing. The daily conversations that he had with customers were opportunities to share love and joy to those who may have woken up on the wrong side of the bed that morning. While Isaiah's job was ultimately to sell as much merchandise as possible, he was able to develop small relationships with customers who would eventually ask things such as "Where are you from? Where do you go to school? What are your goals in life?" Those questions allowed Isaiah to share a little bit about himself and the values that he held, while at the same time making the customer feel relaxed and more likely to purchase items. Isaiah was also able to become cordial with his coworkers, who appreciated his contributions to the team.

People want to follow strong leaders and behaviors, especially when they see positive results. When people ask, "How are you always happy? How do you do your job so well?" we can use people's natural curiosity and inclinations (to seek love and joy) to share the Gospel. Evangelism then becomes much easier for us to do, and in turn we can get others to turn toward God. As society continues to deteriorate, more opportunities will pop up for us to show our high standards. As culture distances itself from all things good and lovely, Christians will naturally elevate themselves. Even if we simply maintain the status quo, we are doing better than the average person. How much more of an impact will we have in the world if we live out the gold standard in accordance with God's will?

If we establish a good attitude and are willing to be used by God, God will allow opportunities to present themselves in whatever industry we are in. This is not only a challenge to yourself, but it provides opportunities that will allow you to perform tangible acts of service that reinforce your personal and philosophical views that ultimately reflect the ideologies of the gold standard.

The way one sets the tone on how people should behave is actually preaching the Gospel in and of itself. One does not need to be on the side of the road with a sign to preach God's Word, but in our actions we will shine a light so others can see the goodness of God.

For those of us that want to follow God and give our all, we need to start with our internal lives, and if that is hard, ask God for help and "fake it until you make it." Let me clarify. The way we live our lives in the public eye is normally how we want to portray ourselves to the world. Meaning, when we hang out with friends, talk to coworkers, and talk to a waiter or a cashier, we need to exemplify the righteousness and the joyfulness of the kingdom of God, even if we don't feel like it. It is hard to always be in the mood to do things to the best of our abilities, but if we push through the hardships, we will eventually get into a cycle of naturally being kind, joyful, and just. Even if you are feeling down in the dumps, it does not mean that you now have the right to make someone else's day worse. We can never fully grasp what other people are going through in their lives, and one positive interaction can save someone from going off the rails and remind others that good still exists in the world, good that is ultimately given to us from God.

Looks Good in Chapel, but Abysmal in Practice

"So wake up, and strengthen what you still have before it dies completely. For I find that what you have done is not yet perfect in the sight of my God." Revelation 3:2 (GNB)

Every Sunday morning at a church near you, there are dozens, hundreds, sometimes thousands of people that sing and proclaim the goodness of God. Unfortunately, when people leave church and head to Sunday brunch, emotions can change quickly from love and adoration of God to hate and disgust toward a waiter that messed up their order. While that is a lighthearted example, there are too many Christians that only praise God's name during Sunday service, Bible study, and holidays (the rest of the days are full of idolatry and immorality and ultimately being a disgrace of a professing Christian). There is also the issue of the youth ultimately walking away from the church due to various reasons (giving in to the desires of the world, the church not having a strong stance on current day issues, and the youth of today not knowing what their place in the church should be). This is not to say that all churches have these issues, but very often the churches that you hear about in the news are the ones that have some issues, to say the least. Time and time again there always seems to be some type of church that is involved in one type of scandal or another

In short, too many Christians are living their lives in a secular manner which is watering down the biblical message at best and destroying the credibility of God's goodness at its worst.

Israelites did not understand their calling in the Old Testament; they didn't fully grasp the fact that they were supposed to be different from the other nations. In Exodus 19:5-6, God had called the Isrealietes to be Holy (set apart) from other nations so that they could be an example to others, but at times the Isrealites would lose sight of God's plan. Instead, they sought to be like other countries and live the lifestyle that others lived, from wishing that they had Egyptian food while wandering in the wilderness, to fornicating with foreigners who led them away from God, to even seeking to have their own kings instead of being ruled by prophets that were led by God

In a similar manner, I think that Christians today don't always understand their calling. If a Christian who was living in sin without remorse went to evangelize to an unbeliever, the unbeliever can simply respond with, "Why would I believe in God when you don't live any differently than I do?"

Our calling is to be a righteous example to others in our conduct and spread God's Word through one of three aspects: Evangelism, teaching, and fellowship/servitude. There are other things that churches can do, but if churches can do at least one of those three things well, they will be set up for success. We are to be different from the norm, which is sometimes where churches get tripped up. You often see churches trying to "Christianize" different things from pop culture in order to try and seem "hip" to the younger generation (that's where you get the "trendy youth pastor" stereotypes), when instead the church's main focus should be to foster a warm environment for families to praise God together, learn more about God's Word, and fellowship and encourage each other to uphold a righteous standard in their individual lives. Churches as of late are more focused on providing emotional encouragement instead of providing substantial ways to build up one's faith and fellowship with God.

There is nothing intrinsically wrong with a "modern" atmosphere at a church, such as fancy light shows, not having a dress code, or having a 45-minute service. But if the church is simply acting as a concert where people come in and sing a couple songs and maybe get an inspiration quote or two before they return back to their everyday hedonistic lives, then that is a watered-down version of what God intended the church to be.

There are a lot of Christians that have the ambition to preach and serve others, but not everyone has the ambition to preach and serve on their own. When there is a strong leader (good or bad), he can inspire others to do bigger things and create a domino effect of action.

That being said, at the end of the day a Christian's walk is between him and God. Meaning, regardless of what other people are doing, a Christian should strive to honor God with all they have. Even if the churches around the individual are not on fire for God, he should not let the church deter him from going all in on the kingdom of God. However, it is much easier for someone to remain passionate about God's kingdom if they are involved in a church community that also promotes the full devotion to being a Believer in Christ.

Too many times we can see instances where churches are focused more on catering to those outside of the church instead of focusing on its members and making sure that they are walking uprightly. As a whole, the Christian church has become diluted with wishy-washy teaching in an attempt to not offend the worldly masses. We see modern pastors who are "reinterpreting" God's Word and preaching that it is okay to live sinful lives and to not grow in our Christian faith.

The church has gone into a habitual state of promoting God's love while compromising some of its beliefs in an attempt to appeal to the masses and widen its base. By its definition, Christianity is controversial to the ways of the world. If you don't accept that, then it will be very difficult and, in some instances, impossible to live a truly godly life.

Sadly, at times we believers don't unite over the truths of God. Instead, we project our own preferences and elements of God's Word. Yes, there are different denominations and secondary theological differences that different churches have, but in terms of the Word of God, we should all believe in roughly the same thing. Direct affiliation with a denomination should communicate different styles of worship and communication, but the Word of God should remain the same. We see various arguments that pop up from time to time such as pre-tribulation vs. post tribulation, what type of music should be played at church, and even the classic debate of free will vs. predestination. Regardless of where a person leans on these topics, as long as you believe that Jesus Christ died for your sins so you can be holy and walk righteously with God according to the Bible, you are a true Christian.

The church can't take a lukewarm stance and allow itself to just partake in status quo messaging, as God wants our undivided obedience. For us to remain distinct from a society that is rapidly running as far away from the Bible as possible, we need to stand firm in our beliefs and values in the context that God intended. Everything stems from our Christian faith. We know that we are reading the Bible correctly when the interpretation of a Bible verse is not in conflict with the teaching of another Bible verse. God's Word may at times come across as paradoxical, but it does not conflict with itself. Some people may argue that at times the Bible is not historically accurate. People can argue the literalness of seven days of creation, the flood, Egyptian Pharaoh timelines, ancestral timelines, and geographic locations, amongst many other things. Human or translation errors can potentially lead to historical inaccuracies that can be debated vigorously, but the very teachings of God have been proven correct time and time over again.

> *"Jesus said that He did not come down to earth to remove the Mosaic laws in the Old Testament but to fulfill the law and give modern day examples on how to live a holy life. He focuses not just on physically walking in righteousness but first reforming our hearts and minds so that we can spiritually walk in righteousness."* *(Matthew 5:17-48)*

Oftentimes, the modern church of today's society focuses on Bible verses such as "Love your neighbor as yourself" and interprets that to mean that Christians should be accepting of the transgenderism movement or hook-up culture in their churches. But, if one truly understands that verse in context with the other verses in the Bible, then they would understand that it is loving to encourage others to walk in righteousness and let them know that Jesus died for them and will forgive them if they turn away from their ways. Most importantly, it is the most loving thing to not misrepresent God's teachings, as that would be lying to others who may have no idea that they are even sinning in the first place. The modern church has strayed from reading the Bible and moved on to catchy phrases and feel-good quotes to make people feel spiritually self-righteous.

Not all mega churches are the "modern church" that we are referring to, although they may be more likely to want to conform to the ways of the world. In reality, it is we Christians who make up the church congregations, the ones that tithe every weekend, the ones who listen to sermons, and the ones who ultimately lead other people to our churches. Because Christians collectively are the church, we need to look at ourselves and see what we individually are standing for.

Lights, Worship, Action

"IF MY PEOPLE WHO ARE CALLED BY MY NAME WILL HUMBLE THEMSELVES, AND PRAY AND SEEK MY FACE, AND TURN FROM THEIR WICKED WAYS, THEN I WILL HEAR FROM HEAVEN, AND WILL FORGIVE THEIR SIN AND HEAL THEIR LAND." 2 CHRONICLES 7:14 (NKJV)

Second Chronicles 7:14 is Isaiah's grandma's life verse, and it is powerful when you dissect it. If we as God's people (believers in God) get rid of our pride and selfishness and draw close to God by asking Him to give us the power to walk in righteousness, then God will forgive us of our shortcomings and will do miraculous works and turn our country around back toward righteous ways.

Christians should be on fire for God in all aspects. Christians should not be in a state of depression no matter how bad the world gets; we are called to bring joy and truth into the world.

We also should not be afraid to call something immoral if it goes against God's word (sexual immorality is one of the biggest things that Christians should be firm on). The church should be a welcoming atmosphere, but once they are a part of the church, members should be required to follow God's rules and not their fleshly desires.

We should continue to be at the forefront of charitable events and community gatherings. This does not have to be a flashy thing; simply being a participant of a social event is a great place to start. Christians do lead the world when it comes to charity, and Liberty University's student requirements of Christian service and other forms of outreach are great places to start. Liberty also talks about the importance of being involved with a church. While it is trendy to do so now, I hope that people are also involved in their church in their respective hometowns. After high school (and college if people go), one's social circle decreases significantly, as school (and maybe clubs or the military) is the only institution where attendees are almost guaranteed to find young people that are around a similar age. This is where the church can come into play. In an ideal society, the church should be at the forefront of a community. If a church is large enough, there should be various events that members can participate in, whether it be a Bible study, youth events, or a food drive. Churches that are smaller can merge activities with other churches in the area to promote cohesion and fellowship with other believers.

Having different activities and opportunities for fellowship allows for members to connect with each other on a deeper level, and it also provides a sense of accountability for members and church leaders. There should be checks and balances within church communities, with everyone's goal being to follow God's Word as closely as possible. Various outlets also can spark creativity and a desire for Christians to pursue various passions and trades, whether that be farming, crafting, or even entertainment. That is one of the biggest reasons we attended Liberty University, as they are on the forefront of Christian excellence from a collegiate level.

When entering college, one of the biggest things on a student's mind is to eventually find a partner to eventually marry (shout out to "Ring by Spring"). Although neither of us is married to a Liberty girl (that is a podcast in and of itself), it is easy to see how so many relationships are formed on campus. Being in the same community allows ample opportunities for interaction and a deeper relationship to naturally foster. Sometimes when a couple gets married, they fail to connect with a community and take on the mantra, "the two of us against the world." That can be a dangerous mentality, as Christian communities can help reduce some of the main issues that can come up in marriages. Looking at Divorce.com's "Top 10 Marriage Failure Reasons," the biggest three reasons for marital divorces are financial burdens/undisclosed debts, trouble opening up with their spouse, and running a family. Let's address those three reasons.

Financial discomfort, although a shallow reason for divorce, is a common occurrence whether in or out of marriage. If a married couple is a part of a loving community, oftentimes members will step in and aid the couple (new or old) with things such as a baby shower, offering meals and hand-me-down clothes, and will even help with miscellaneous things such as tutoring or babysitting, and even with DIY projects around the house. The community can also point people in the right direction when it comes to managing finances and saving money. It may not be ideal, but a marriage should be able to financially survive if they are willing to reach out for help when needed.

This may be a stretch, but I believe that being an active participant in one's community forces active communication. For example, if there is a church picnic occurring on a Saturday, the married couple will have to communicate and plan what they are bringing to the picnic, how long will they stay there, and discuss any other arrangements that need to be made. Now that all sounds pretty surface level, but when there are constant and positive conversations occurring at a lighter level, it makes it easier to delve into deep conversations such as life goals, dreams, fears, etc. Also, when one starts making friendships with other members in the community, he or she is more likely to start conversing about deeper things with other community members. That in and of itself should cause more conversations to occur with one's spouse. For example, after church is over and a married couple is home, a normal conversation starter such as "how was your day?" can easily start a conversation on the different occurrences that happened that day, such as talking with the pastor about a theological question, having a sports debate with a friend, or how good the meal was after the service.

Being in a community makes it much easier to seek advice on how to raise a family, and a community can also help take off the pressure of raising kids entirely on your own.

Christian community is built as a safety net to help everyone in the community get on their feet and stay on their feet. Being in a community makes it harder to not be an outcast or a loner, as when you isolate yourself, normally someone in the community notices (and will reach out, in theory). The church community is not something that should be abused (in theory, if everyone is walking righteously then there should not be any problems, but things happen sometimes), and if there is cause for concern then the church leaders can address it.

Christians have done a good job with joining movements such as the pro-life movement.

During the Trump administration, the pro-life movement gained traction from a majority of spiritual leaders combining forces to project a united front against the evils of abortion and being able to promote Judeo-Christian principles on a national scale. And that movement is still going strong today. Christians are also on the forefront when it comes to charity, from donating their time and energy serving those in homeless shelters, giving resources to food banks, and even founding large corporations like the Salvation Army.

We should continue to champion our viewpoints in the public square and not be afraid of pushback from the world. It is okay if they are not accepting of our views, as many people were not accepting of Jesus when He was on earth. We need to humbly but boldly proclaim Christ's love for all, and that can easily be done through acts of service, working hard in our daily vocations, our friendships and acquaintances, and even in entertainment.

It is easy for Christians to get involved in community service; churches often have different outreach opportunities that they do on a weekly or monthly basis. If churches do not have anything, then Christians should look to contribute at community centers, schools, and other public places such as being a volunteer fireman. God has given everyone all sorts of interests and skill sets, and it is a wonderful thing when we can share those gifts with others.

The easiest change in our lives will be to put more effort into tasks that we already do. It is good to take on an extra task, stay later an extra hour, or complete additional training to assist whatever business that you are working on. These things can be done without overloading one's workload. People notice those with ambition, and when you partner the trait ambition with good work, then coworkers will have a positive relationship with you. Being able to have a positive relationship with your coworkers and supervisors allows you to be more comfortable talking about life at work. Sometimes, people do not want to be bothered or have a busy schedule and do not have time for conversations. If that is the case for some people, then we as Christians should not be bothersome to others when it comes to making conversation. But, if there is an opportunity to converse with others, we should not be bashful to talk about God and godly principles. Maybe people will talk about the news and the different trending topics, maybe people are comfortable with talking about politics and theology, or maybe someone wants to talk about what is going on in their individual lives and just wants someone to listen to them. Whatever the scenario is, we should be led by God and interact (or not interact) with them and be a blessing to them, not a curse.

When Christians get into the public spheres of entertainment such as TV shows, video games, movies, and social media, we need to make sure that we are not giving up godly principles in order to market to others. Sometimes Christian movies are trying too hard to be secular, and some movie critics are sometimes wanting secular things from a Christian perspective. For example, some Christian movie critics may want to see the scandal of a soap opera or the racy scenes that often accompany romance movies, but hey, everyone turns to worship Jesus at the end! People are coming in with the wrong expectations on entertainment; they are seeking to find worldly and fleshly desires from a movie that should be spiritually uplifting. Those types of movie scenes are not beneficial to Christians as we should not be showing or viewing content that is sinful. There are ways to get a point across without showing obscenity, such as dimming lights, subtle transitioning, and closing of doors.

Striking a balance of people sinning and making mistakes versus resisting temptation and walking uprightly is a hard thing to do. Let me explain. We should be promoting movies that resist temptation, but I see how it is good to show what happens (or what can happen) if people fall into sin. In general, it is refreshing to watch actors flee from evil, and it can show viewers good tactics to avoid falling into sin. We should normalize righteousness in movies, not make it a rare occurrence.

That being said, it is good to note that God's redeeming love applies to all, even to those who have strayed from Him. Movements such as purity culture had a tendency to completely shun those who had fallen into lustful temptations, instead of focusing on God forgiving them if they turned from their wrongdoings. Movies do a good job of showing turning points in a person's life, and they allow us to really pinpoint the exact moment that someone fell into sin. Those movies can help Christians examine their own lives and stop themselves from a bad trajectory. A good example of this is the movie "Freshman Year" which portrays the struggles of a young Christian adult that is on his own at college and has to make life-changing decisions. It shows the man resisting temptations, and it also shows him falling into sin, but most importantly the movie does not focus on the sin but instead focuses on God's grace and forgiveness as well as the work that God does in the young man's family. A big thing that Christian movie directors need to remember is to not go over the top and show unnecessary filler scenes about sin. Sometimes it feels like screenwriters and viewers are having the following thoughts: "Yes, they fell into temptation. But let's watch and see JUST how much they fell into temptation..." as the camera zooms in on the actors doing unholy acts.

If one watches fornication, cursing, stealing, and lying all the time, how can we be sure that those things won't try and creep into our lives? Scenes from movies, video games, and social media often float about our thoughts, sometimes our dreams, and sometimes they cause us to act or speak in a certain way. An example of this is in the music that we listen to. 99.9% of people at some point in their lives will catch themselves humming a tune, singing a phrase, or quoting words from a song. The content of the music we are listening to can seep into our subconscious, and if left unchecked, it can lead to outward actions.

Christians cannot blame everything on the church; we all have individual, personal relationships with God, and we need to have personal accountability. Before we shame others in how they are acting, we need to check our own actions and see where we should repent and where we can walk more in the fruits of the Spirit.

If Christians truly unite to establish a gold standard, there will actually be effective and widespread progress in advancing morality and implementing the gold standard in everyday life, which we are outlining in this book. It starts in our churches, but we need to make sure that the standard does not stay there; we need to apply it to all aspects of our lives.

Titus 2 is a great blueprint on the roles that the church should be doing. It is good to read the entire chapter, but in this book I want to focus on verses six through eight which says the following:

> *"Likewise, exhort the young men to be sober-minded, in all things showing yourself to be a pattern of good works; in doctrine showing integrity, reverence, incorruptibility, sound speech that cannot be condemned, that one who is an opponent may be ashamed, having nothing evil to say of you." Titus 2:6-8 (NKJV)*

As our book is focused on the youth, we can follow these teachings from the Bible by being hardworking individuals with a high sense of morality and respect for righteous values. When we walk in righteousness and promote godly ideals, then those who oppose us will be standing up for debased, inhumane, and degrading principles that the average person despises. Unfortunately, this world is trending further and further away from godly values, which is why we now get into some of the pushback that an outspoken Christian may face in life.

Occupational Hazards of a Christian

As basketball enthusiasts, we like to compare today's social and spiritual climate to an intense basketball game with the home team leading by two points in the 4th quarter, but the away team's crowd is really into the game and more energetic and invested in their team's success than the home crowd. In this same manner, Christian values in Western society are barely hanging on by a thread. The fact that our God-given rights are still be observed in America proves that we still have godly values, but the opposition is currently putting in more time, effort, and even money to do their best to erase the "lead" that Christians have held for centuries in the west.

The reasons why the home team fans aren't as hyped as the away team fans can vary. Either the home team fans are too discouraged to cheer as their lead is fading away, or they don't want to come across as obnoxious, or worse, "offensive." Either that or the game is not that important to them, and they just want the game to be over. Do you see the correlation to the "home team fans" and believers in our society?

We don't want to fight fire with fire, but you cannot just watch the fire burn your house down either. We want to stand firm and preach God's Word to the masses, but we want you all to be aware that standing up for your beliefs may cause extra challenges to your life.

Because Christians are called to a higher standard, there is more pressure to perform at a higher rate. If Christians accidentally sin, there is usually a swifter punishment for the Christian than for another person (this makes sense in a way as we do not want to come across as hypocrites). They are also easy targets of hate as people think that Christians are close-minded. Society used to distance itself from people who were morally debased and went against the most basic Judeo-Christian values, but as morality becomes more and more subjective, society has turned into cancel-culture that basically seeks to de-platform those who are intolerant of another person's views (generally speaking). Spiritual warfare is not only real but also ramping up on Christians due to the fact that the opposition is doing its best to discourage Christians in the end days.

Christians in eastern civilizations have been strongly persecuted for their faith for centuries, with people being stripped away from their homelands and their families and sentenced to prison camps or to be martyred. While we are extremely thankful that this is not happening on a widespread scale in the west, we do want to remind our readers that being a Christian is not always easy in our day-to-day lives.

Christian language has been polluted, from the rainbow symbol and the phrase "eye for an eye" to mean perverted things such as pedophilic movements to extreme cases of reparations, and re-sanctifying that language is very difficult to do (look at the "Take Back the Rainbow Movement"). Buzzwords and phrases such as "love is love" and "live and let live" are often used to stop people from shaming other people's life choices. Those phrases are meant to come across as well-intended, but when a better alternative option is provided, it is shut down because the opinion is "hateful," "condescending," or bigoted." Even stating Christian beliefs in the public square such as modesty and vows of chastity can lead to hateful reactions, and if you are outspoken on topics such as marriage being between a man and a woman, then you can be in legal trouble.

Tim Tebow is a name that many football fans will recognize as one of the most polarizing figures in the National Football League (NFL). His football career, marked by both wins and losses, is not the only thing that made him stand out during his time in the NFL. One of the things that made him a standout player was his unwavering faith in God, a faith that he was not afraid to express on and off the field.

First and foremost, Tim Tebow's faith in God was one of the defining features of his football career. As a devout Christian, he wore his faith on his sleeve, on and off the field. His signature move, the "Tebow-ing" pose, where he knelt in prayer after making a touchdown, became famous both in the NFL and around the world. Through this gesture, he showed his gratitude to God for his success on the field and his faith in the Lord.

Additionally, Tim Tebow's faith often inspired his fellow players and fans as well. It was not uncommon for him to give away his game-used equipment, sign autographs, meet with fans after games, and even visit children's hospitals to spend time with sick children. His charitable work was a testament to his faith in God, and he was always quick to give thanks to his Creator for the blessings he received.

Tim Tebow's influence reached far beyond the football field as well. He was a man of deep faith and integrity, and he never hesitated to speak his mind when it mattered most. This was most evident during his time as a quarterback for the Denver Broncos. The team was struggling, and the fans were losing hope in the team's ability to win games. However, Tim Tebow remained steadfast in his faith and sense of purpose, and he never lost faith in himself or his team.

Moreover, Tim Tebow was an ambassador of Christianity during his time in the NFL. He often shared his testimony with others, both on and off the field, and his message of faith and perseverance reached millions of people around the world. He also used his platform to support various Christian causes and organizations, such as the Tim Tebow Foundation which helps children with life-threatening illnesses and World Vision which aims to alleviate poverty. Through these efforts, Tim Tebow has made a significant impact on the world, both as a football player and as a Christian.

The influence of Christianity that Tim Tebow had during his football career cannot be overstated. He was a man of deep faith and integrity, and he never hesitated to express his beliefs and his gratitude to God. His influence reached far beyond the football field, inspiring fans and fellow players alike, and making a positive impact on people's lives. His legacy as a football player and Christian ambassador will continue to live on, and he will always be remembered as a man of faith, courage, and perseverance.

Tim Tebow is an example of a football player who received extra criticism on his performance mainly due to his outspoken faith, even though he won a lot of clutch games for the Denver Broncos.

Many people may blame his mechanics, but we think that he would have had a long career, similar to David Carr, if he was not as vocal in his faith. (Carr had weird throwing mechanics and far less accolades than Tim Tebow, but he was in the NFL for 11 seasons compared to Tebow's career which was under 5 years.) When the Broncos traded Tim Tebow, he was no longer in an optimal environment for success, and teams did not want to sign him to avoid controversy.

This may be a small example of persecution, and it is still heavily debated whether his performance or persecution caused him to not last long in the NFL. That being said, I think that the things that we promote all have an effect on our lives in the public square and the way society treats us. There are certain positions of power, prestige, and influence that are harder to get into with Christian morals. It is much harder to be a Christian in Hollywood than it is to be a Christian in suburbia, due to the things that Hollywood promotes being in direct conflict with the teachings of God. (The lust of the eyes, lust of the flesh, and the pride of life. 1 John 2:16)

Living out your Christian faith and projecting that in the workplace in our current environment is not easy and definitely comes with hardship and persecution. Our society has begun to turn away from morality and reject those who would want to influence their environment using their faith and the convictions that flow from it. As our culture continues to ramp up hostility against the Judeo-Christian faith and those who seek to use our cultural avenues as platforms to project God's truth and grace, the forces of evil seek to disrupt any pushback and tighten the capability of this from being carried out successfully. Over the last few years, we have seen severe discrimination in the workplace against believers, and the media and other entertainment sectors are beginning to betray Christianity in a hostile and condescending manner. They have begun to mock prayer, reevaluate how the family unit is defined, and disregard the importance of the Judeo-Christian faith on which our country was founded and ultimately why we are allowed to live in this great country.

Our public school system has ramped up its indoctrination of our children and has begun to transform[1] [2] our educational systems to project principles that -completely contradict the Christian faith. [3] [4] Evolution is already a widespread philosophy that is now uniformed throughout most public schools in this nation, completely dismissing the idea of creation and the truth about how the world was formed. We see the increasing support for LGBTQ, trans, and gay initiatives as a great threat. It's not only the images that are being portrayed in front of our children, but the LGBTQ ideology seeks to dismantle a family unit. Once our society begins to redefine marriage and how a family was intended to operate, it compromises not only society's ability to succeed as a whole and tears down the moral fabric of a nation.

Christian businesses have begun to be ridiculed for promoting basic beliefs and principles articulated in the Scriptures. We have seen Chick-fil-A, a very successful nationwide fast-food chain, be mocked, ridiculed, and even boycotted because of their steadfast belief in not supporting gay rights and for them honoring God by being closed on Sundays. We see athletes being mocked for giving glory to God after victories are playing on the field. An example of this was when Tim Tebow played on the Denver Broncos and used his unique football ability to give glory to God and to ensure that America knew where his success came from and ultimately why he pursued playing in the NFL. During Tebow's tenure, Christians united around him, not because of his Denver Broncos uniform, but because of the Christian faith that he projected and unashamedly preached on the national level as he was quarterback and led them to the postseason. He exemplified compassion and generosity as he supported many organizations that assist the less fortunate and those without a voice, from the Super Bowl commercial that he starred in with him mom to actively creating the Tim Tebow Foundation that was decide to help others, people can see the genuine love for God that Tebow and his family has. Despite all of those things that he did, he received pushback from activists and large organizations. When Tebow prayed and thanked God after he scored a touchdown, the NFL frowned upon Tebow making his faith public.

In the media we see a multitude of Christian conservatives being silenced and ridiculed for the proclamation of their faith in the beliefs that they seek to communicate to their audience on a national level, whether it's Fox News, CNN, or MSNBC, the message is clear that they seek to remove the Judeo-Christian faith from the entertainment and media arena. So what is the media replacing Christian values with? Let's talk about that in the next chapter.

Tom Brady and the Worldly Standard

"DO NOT LOVE THE WORLD OR THE THINGS IN THE WORLD. IF ANYONE LOVES THE WORLD, THE LOVE OF THE FATHER IS NOT IN HIM. FOR ALL THAT IS IN THE WORLD——THE LUST OF THE FLESH, THE LUST OF THE EYES, AND THE PRIDE OF LIFE——IS NOT OF THE FATHER BUT IS OF THE WORLD. AND THE WORLD IS PASSING AWAY, AND THE LUST OF IT; BUT HE WHO DOES THE WILL OF GOD ABIDES FOREVER." 1 JOHN 2:15-17 (NKJV)

We would be kidding ourselves if we said that living according to the world's standards did not come with certain benefits. Although they are shallow compared to the gold standard of righteousness, the benefits of following your carnal desires are that you will get immediate feelings of gratification as you can do whatever you want whenever you want, and your guilt will eventually fade away as your indulgences continue. You will seldom be persecuted for standing up for good, because your version of "good" aligns with the modern-day viewpoint. You can also be more selfish and try to gain notoriety through debased things (although if you do not believe in the Bible, you may consider debased things to be "wholesome") or get rich from deception, selfishness, and in some cases through theft.

Not having to appeal to a moral authority other than the government can be freeing for a time, and you may be able to achieve more goals that you have in life. Hollywood celebrities, musical artists, supermodels, and high-ranking government officials are mostly non-Christian believers, and that is not purely coincidental. Because of sin entering the world, people are innately drawn toward the desires of being free to live however they would like, and some people are keener on rebelling against those in authoritative positions (such as parents, teachers, and pastoral leaders). Curiosity that is not kept in check can lead people on dangerous paths toward the dark spiritual realm. Ironically, some people use magic to become famous, as you hear of people selling their souls to the devil in exchange for earthly pleasures. Let's take a look at some popular people and see how they may have been impacted by chasing after the things of the world.

Tom Brady (the person who ended Tim Tebow's magical playoff run ironically) is widely considered the GOAT (Greatest of All Time) of football. (As Isaiah is an avid Miami Dolphins fan, he is compelled to disagree with that claim of GOAT status.) Most people know that Tom Brady has had three separate hall of fame campaigns all in one football career. As a quarterback in the NFL, Tom Brady has set numerous records for both individual and group accomplishments. He holds the record for the most NFL titles won by a single player (7), the most Super Bowl appearances (10) and wins (7), and the most MVP awards (5). In addition, he has the most career yards, completions, touchdown passes, games started, and victories in the NFL. He has the most division titles (17), AFC Championship Games (13), and playoff games (34) won by any player and has never had a losing season. He is the only Super Bowl MVP to have played for both two different teams as he won the titles when he was playing for the New England Patriots and the Tampa Bay Buccaneers. He played for 23 seasons in the NFL, even though he was the 199th pick in his draft class in the 2000 draft. Many people thought that he would retire many years before he actually did in 2023, and the jury is still out on whether he will stay retired for good or if he will pull the same stunt that he did in 2022.

Tom Brady has all of the accolades, praises, and fortunes that a mere mortal man can simply dream of, but off the field is he winning in life? His family has split as he and his wife have divorced. Interestingly, it is common knowledge that Tom Brady's ex-wife Giselle Bündchen is a practicing witch and performed rituals on Tom Brady, and some people speculate if his wife used her witchcraft to grant Tom Bray the ability to perform and exceed expectations. Whether divination caused Tom Brady to be the best football player of all time or not, it is interesting to note that the devil is interested in helping people succeed in their lives, in exchange for compensation of some kind, such as the disruption of a stable family unit. Some people theorize that the divorce happened because of Brady constantly being away playing football, but Giselle denies the rumors, although they are partly true.

In a Bazaar interview, Giselle claimed that Brady's demanding football schedule (and the fact that he may not have spent as much time at home as she would have wanted) "is one piece of a much bigger puzzle." Giselle states that "sometimes you grow together; sometimes you grow apart" in reference to their divorce, and that they wanted different things in life, such as chasing their different career paths. Whatever the circumstances were that lead to the divorce, it is more than likely that a demonic presence was involved with Tom Brady's family affairs. People do not divorce because they "love each other too much." Divorce generally occurs from one spouse or both either cheating in the relationship, being abusive, or being selfish. It seems like Giselle wanted to divorce because of the latter (selfishness), as she wanted to continue chasing her career regardless of the potential impact it would have on her children, who are around 10 and 13 years old. The devil is the "father of lies," and people are lying to themselves if they think that a no-fault divorce will bring them true happiness.

Giselle admitted that it felt like a part of her had "died" and that she was going through a "rebirth," and although she misses some aspects of her marriage, she still feels like her and Brady are still working together. "We're not playing against each other," Giselle said of her and Brady. "We are a team, and that's beautiful. I look back and I have no regrets. I loved every bit of it." That statement really does not make any sense if one thinks about it for long enough. The definition of divorce literally means to terminate a marital union, which is breaking up the tightest team in the world: a strong marriage. If her and Tom Brady were really a team, they could have worked out how they could both continue to chase their passions while remaining an intact family. It seems like they just wanted to date other people, but they failed to understand that marriage is a covenant relationship that is supposed to last a lifetime. Sadly, although Tom Brady grew up in a Catholic household, his strong values either deteriorated or never existed in the first place, as he seldom mentions his faith anymore. Celeb Answers Writer Sandra Robinson stated the following:

> "Despite his upbringing in a Catholic household, Brady has not officially revealed that he is religious. The early years of Brady's career showed that he had stayed true to his faith, however as the years passed, Brady seems to have gone astray from his Catholic roots to follow another path."

Now it must be prefaced that we will never fully know what is going on in an individual's spiritual life (even celebrities), but the Bible does say that we can judge others based on their actions. Although Tom Brady has not spoken an official statement on his divorce, it seems like he is mutually okay with the divorce occurring and has no regrets on the longevity of his football career based on his comments and actions. While he has all the recognition that some would kill for, will his lifestyle lead to lasting and eternal happiness?

Let's talk about another celebrity that got caught up in the limelight.

Meghan Markle dreamed of becoming a true princess, but when she actually became one, she instantly regretted it. Although Meghan was raised as a Christian, she was involved in "Hollywood" TV shows and productions for most of her life, and being in that environment promoted selfishness, pride, envy, and other hedonistic traits. Meghan was cast in different shows looking to elevate herself, which in and of itself is a great ambition to have, but she chose roles that did not align with her Christian faith. Meghan herself said that she felt she was being "reduced to a bimbo" on one of the game shows that she modeled for and acted in some unwholesome scenes in an attempt to make a name for herself.

After a marriage and a divorce, she eventually marries Prince Harry of England, and they have a lovely wedding that exceeds all of her expectations. They begin to start their happily ever after on the perfect note. Meghan now has the fame of being the first "outsider" to marry into the royal family, the status that she has chased for years, and the luxuries that come with the title of being a "princess."

It is crazy that despite all of the prestige that the Parliament and British royalty had to offer, it was not enough for Markle to feel loved, valued, or even recognized. Instead, she felt hated and ostracized by jealous onlookers, and she and her husband claim that certain family members purposely gave the British media hit pieces to write about her. Most of the drama seems to be rather petty, but nonetheless the drama was piling up.

Unfortunately, the drama that ensued led to her and her husband leaving the royal family so they could be "free" from the drama. Meghan Markle had been around drama her entire life in Hollywood, and now she finally had enough, "allegedly." Unfortunately, instead of living a private life and truly staying out of the limelight, Meghan saw an opportunity to generate more fame and some additional revenue by airing out all of the British royalty's dirty secrets, whether the claims were true or not. The television environment that she was in naturally led her to constantly seeking validation from others, so much so that even when she claimed that she was done with the fame, she was enticed back into it. The worldly standard is all about promoting oneself and constantly making a name for oneself, even if that means putting others down. The entertainment industry is cutthroat for a reason, as drama and scandals run rampant to garner attention.

People also do not have long attention spans, as people will be invested in one actress for a season, and then move on to the next. The same goes with the shows and movies that people watch, different interviews, and even in-person events. We are in the height of the information age, and literally everyone is seeking to be famous, not just in Hollywood but on TikTok, Instagram, YouTube, and many other platforms. While it is nice to be able to access billions of different personalities, interests, and content, sometimes we can get so caught up in the attention-grabbing media frenzy so that we get lost in the sauce and forget the most important things of life. We need to focus on improving ourselves instead of seeking superficial validation from others. Sometimes it is okay to be shunned by the world, and sometimes we should live our lives in the exact opposite way that most people recommend. That brings us to one of the most polarizing celebrities in recent years, the man, the myth, the legend: Andrew Tate.

Andrew Tate and other rich people with similar viewpoints embrace their polarizing status to garner support from those who are tired of the mainstream media and the feminist agenda, which is to deconstruct family values and gender roles and to make them an abstract and subjective concept. Tate is part of the red pill movement that is rapidly growing; the values that the red pill movement promotes are being able to have a strong physique and a sharp mind to be able to succeed in life, whether that success is rooted in sports, business, and relationships.

Now there are different segments of the red pill movement, which is under the umbrella of the manosphere, and the segments can take people down several "rabbit holes." From an outsider's perspective, it is refreshing to see the promotion of men stepping up and being leaders in society as well as starting the pushback against the narrative that women should be promiscuous. However, some parts of the red pill movement take things way too far, with some people saying that men can sleep around with as many women as they want because they are "high value men," and some people in the movement can inversely be promoting the degradation and manipulation of women. At times, it seems like men and women are now ferociously attacking each other with no real appreciation of the roles that each person is supposed to play in life.

Andrew Tate became famous for being a strong kickboxer and for making viral comments on how to talk to women (some people think that he is misogynistic and discriminatory towards women, but we won't get into that in depth). Part of the comments he makes are just to get people to click on his content and watch and think for themselves.

Andrew Tate used to be an orthodox Christian, but he is now a practicing Muslim. Ironically, the viewpoints that he held have almost always been centered towards Islam beliefs, especially on the way that he looks at and treats women. He hates the fact that there are large sectors of women who are no longer wanting to be in committed relationships, and he hates that men are losing their masculinity and are lazily going through the motions in their lives without self-improvement. He quickly gained a large following as people loved his frankness and longed for an alternative perspective to the mainstream media's propaganda of sedating people to give into their cravings and indulgences. Unfortunately, with Andrew Tate, he does have some concerning things that are happening in his life that may raise questions. While this book is being written, Andrew Tate is currently in house arrest under the suspicion of human trafficking (he has fervently denied the charges and there is no concrete proof he has done anything illegal at the moment), and Tate himself used to run different adult content sites and gladly took on clients that wished to sell their bodies in exchange for fame and money. He profited off of the same morals that he is against. Andrew Tate says that he is under attack by those who hate his message, which is definitely true, but it would have been even easier for Tate to have avoided certain allegations by not getting involved in those immoral industries in the first place. There are a lot of great statements and values that Andrew Tate has, but viewers should always filter what he says and make sure his viewpoints match with the Word of God. That being said, Andrew Tate's webcamming business occurred ten years ago, and Andrew Tate is distancing himself from some of his past behaviors and is promoting morality and religion to his viewers, and it is refreshing to see a celebrity promote good values.

It is interesting to note that Tom Brady, Meghan Markle, and Andrew Tate all have had a Christian background at some point in their lives but were corrupted by the different lusts of the world that are heavily ingrained in the lifestyles of the rich and famous. Andrew Tate seems to be leaning more towards religion in general, although he is leaning more towards Islam rather than Christianity. All three of these celebrities all have great skill sets and a strong work ethic, but good quality traits such as ambition and discipline can become dangerous if the things that one is striving for are bad. Even the philosophy that the self-improvement movement teaches (Dress nicely, go to the gym, get money and girls and fame will come) isn't perfect as those things do not truly make one happy, and we can talk about the endless amounts of stories of rich and famous people being depressed, empty, and lonely. Oftentimes fame and money do not last, and even if it does last, people are still not satisfied. Below are a few quotes of celebrities who wish they weren't famous:

Kristen Stewart (actress)

"Fame is the worst thing in the world...especially if it's pointless. When people say, 'I want to be famous' – why? You don't do anything?"

Justin Bieber (singer)

"People see the glam and the amazing stuff, but they don't know the other side. This life can rip you apart."

Keira Knightley (actress)

"I hate red-carpet events. I absolutely hate them... You have this feeling that everyone wants a bit of you...every photo takes away a bit of your soul. I wish I was just an insignificant speck."

Mary-Kate Olsen (Actress)

"I look at old photos of me, and I don't feel connected to them at all. I would never wish my upbringing on anyone..."

Time and time again we hear from celebrities who talk about how hard their life is and how they wish to have a "normal life" or a sense of belonging outside of their talents and wealth. It goes to show how the Bible is proven true time and time again with Mark 8:36 saying, "For what shall it profit a man, if he shall gain the whole world, and lose his own soul?" (KJV)

The phrase "selling one's soul" is so commonplace now in Hollywood that it is expected for people to give up their morality (and in extreme cases their mortality).

*"My family is under attack by Satan, I'm scared for daughter Miley." – **Billy Ray Cyrus on Miley Cyrus***

*"I signed a deal with Satan because I wanted to get famous. Then I forgot I had a deal with Satan and then I got really famous." – **Roseanne Barr***

*"I'm selling my soul to Hollywood Records. I love you like a love song baby, a sinful miracle, lyrical. He ate my soul. He's Lucifer. I'm torn; I'm selling my soul to the rhythm because I've become so possessed with the music he plays. I chose a path and I'm not looking back." – **Selena Gomez***

It is saddening to see what people will do to achieve fame and fortune, but it is also a sobering reminder of what people will do if they do not value those things more than their lives or the lives of their family members and friends. People who steal and murder for financial gain are often blinded by their desires to get rich quick, and when they look back at their lives, they have no idea how they turned into a monster. If people are willing to partake in random dares doing things that they would never want to do for a quick $20, it makes sense how people rationalize things and end up doing something drastic like selling their body and soul for money. I mean, people will work in jobs that they hate with every fiber of their bone as long as it brings in those sweet, sweet Benjamin Franklins.

Why do people want money so badly? Well, it fixes a lot of problems. People obviously need money for food, clothing, and shelter, and people often want to create "generational wealth" so that their families and business can be taken care of when they are gone. People often feel like money is needed to satisfy deeper desires as well, such as happiness, pleasure, entertainment, and experiences that they would not be able to have if it wasn't for money. The things that money can do for a person are seemingly infinite; you can travel the world, go on fancy vacations, eat at fancy restaurants, buy real estate, and change the world for better or for worse. It is true that money can do all of these things, but when looking at the ultra-rich, despite their lifestyles, some of them still seem unfulfilled in life, even after they've acquired more money than 75% of the world. That being said, there are also a good amount of wealthy people that are happy.

Here are some quotes from a BusinessInsider article that talks about why billionaires are happier than the average person.

"Money doesn't change one's ability to be happy – it magnifies your personality." **– Simon Cooper**

"Billionaires have choices, opportunities, and strong relationships — all three of which make them happy." **– Rafael Badziag**

People that are happy get happier when they get richer, and likewise people that are unhappy get less happy when they get more money. If a man who does not have many friends suddenly becomes rich, he will constantly be suspicious when others try to be his friend. He will most likely think that people only want to hang out with him just for his money. Does that mean that having money or being famous is bad? Of course not; it depends on what people do with the money or the fame. Job and Solomon were filthy rich, and David and Jesus Himself were some of the most famous men in their respective time periods. What matters is that you recognize who allows you to have fame and fortune and to use those two things to further God's Kingdom. Solomon built the most beautiful temples, and his downfall was women (surprisingly not his greed for fame or riches).

Having money does make life easier in certain circumstances (you can argue that money can also make life more difficult, but we won't cover that in this book). Oftentimes people say that "money is the root of evil," but if one truly reads the Bible passage that the phrase comes from, they will see that it says the "love" of money is the root of evil (as in the lust after money).

The desire to be famous is also not an evil thing in and of itself, but what you do with the fame is what determines whether the fame is a net negative or a net positive. There also could be a reason why you are not famous, as perhaps God knows that the fame may be too much for us to handle at the moment.

The Bible says that we should do everything unto God (1 Corinthians 10:31), which means that we should use any fame that we may have to point others to God.

Now the reason that we talked about these celebrities is not to ridicule them just because they are famous but to show Christians who are seeking fame and fortune that if we focus solely on earthly treasures and lose sight of relying on God to bring us happiness and contentedness, then the lives we live will be unfulfilling. We should be ambitious and strive to be the best we can be in all aspects of our lives, but if we are not directing our work unto the Lord, then we can end up being overcome by our sinful desires.

Before we wag our fingers at people who are caught up in the rich and famous lifestyle, we need to check our own hearts and make sure there are not conceited desires that we are caught up in. The following verse is a sober reminder for all of us to make sure we are holding ourselves accountable to the gold standard before we chastise others:

> *"Judge not, that you be not judged. For with what judgment you judge, you will be judged; and with the measure you use, it will be measured back to you. And why do you look at the speck in your brother's eye, but do not consider the plank in your own eye? Or how can you say to your brother, 'Let me remove the speck from your eye'; and look, a plank is in your own eye? Hypocrite! First remove the plank from your own eye, and then you will see clearly to remove the speck from your brother's eye."*
> *Matthew 7:1-5 (NKJV)*

So, how should we treat celebrities who are not following God's ways? What about celebrities who are principled Christians? How should we look at the entertainment industry as a whole; should we boycott all types of entertainment like sports, video games, social media, and all genres of movies? After all, it is hard to find Christian celebrities in modern culture, but they are there if one looks hard enough and long enough. And there are non-Christian celebrities that are a net positive in society, from the charitable donations, sponsor-ships, and acts of service that the rich give. (After all, someone needs to be able to pay for the nonprofits to stay afloat.) In terms of the entertainment industry, at the very least there are hundreds, maybe thousands of different genres and forms of entertainment. It would be very hard to give up all of those things that make us happy and keep us entertained. Well, let's get into all of those questions.

In terms of the entertainment industry, as long as the entertainment itself is pleasing to God, then it is perfectly fine to partake in it. Adult entertainment such as pornography should not be viewed by Christians as it is immoral and against God's will. Jesus Himself says it very clearly in the Bible.

> *"You have heard that it was said to those of old, 'You shall not commit adultery.' But I say to you that whoever looks at a woman to lust for her has already committed adultery with her in his heart." Matthew 5:27-28 (NKJV)*

But what about entertainment that is not blatantly adult content? Now, it is very hard to get away from sexual content in the entertainment industry (and just in society) as a whole, as there are suggestive outfits that women often wear on the red carpet, to video games appealing to the male gaze, to even some sports teams that are endorsing their cheerleaders to seductively get the fans' attention. What should we do? Well, we should do our best to avoid temptations as much as possible, and people have different temptations that can trigger them. I recommend not watching certain shows and turning away from commercials that glorify sexual promiscuity, focusing on the sports game and not on the cheerleaders, and not searching certain topics on the internet. And in some cases, we should forgo certain entertainment altogether if it is a stumbling block. If we are walking with God, then the Holy Spirit will guide us and help us determine whether it is worth watching the entertainment. 1 Corinthians 6 is a great chapter to read in its entirety (it talks about settling disputes among fellow Christians instead of going public and making an unnecessary scene, as well as glorifying God in our daily lives), but verse 12 is really relevant to this topic.

> *"All things are lawful for me, but all things are not helpful. All things are lawful for me, but I will not be brought under the power of any." 1 Corinthians 6:12 (NKJV)*

Technically speaking, the entertainment industry is not inherently evil, and it is lawful to enjoy different pastimes. However, some things are not beneficial to the Christian walk, so we should not allow those things to deter us from following the gold standard that God has set forth for us.

In terms of celebrities who are Christian or those who are promoting Christian acts such as charity and servitude, we should rightfully applaud those who are standing for goodness, even if they don't know that they are doing something "godly" or have ulterior motives. For example, earlier in 2023, Mr. Beast surprisingly received pushback for helping one thousand blind people see for the first time as people blamed him for being "disingenuous" and "exploiting" the people for views. Regardless of his intentions, we should not shame him for doing good deeds. If a social media influencer gets millions of views promoting godly values, then we should celebrate that. People like Donald Trump speaking at a pro-life march is a wonderful thing, regardless of whether Donald Trump is the ideal Christian or not. We should also promote Christian celebrities who blaze their own trails in entertainment, with people such as David A.R White creating Pureflix, Phil Vischer and Mike Nawrocki creating Veggie Tales, Adam Ford creating the Babylon Bee, and thousands of other people and platforms. The sport that Dr. Naismith (who was a Christian chaplain and sports coach) designed which affectionately became known as basketball, was created to give boys at the YMCA an opportunity to play sports in a confined indoor space. Although Christian "influencers" pale in comparison to worldly influencers who make more money and generate more publicity, if not for the Christians, the culture would be vastly worse. We should endorse those who are representing the values that we stand for and also hold fellow Christian celebrities accountable to maintain those values. We should address Christian enterprises, especially if they seem to be turning away from godly standards, or if they make a mistake here and there.

Diversity Equals the Same Truth

"JUST AS A BODY, THOUGH ONE, HAS MANY PARTS, BUT ALL ITS MANY PARTS FORM ONE BODY, SO IT IS WITH CHRIST." 1 CORINTHIANS 12:12 (NIV)

In today's society, people often perceive one of the biggest problems in society to be systemic racism. They think mass shootings, growing poverty and homelessness rates, educational failures, rising insurance and mortgage rates, the "glass ceiling," and ultimately moral issues as a whole are caused by racism or segregation in some way, shape, or form. They think that to solve these problems, everyone just needs to love one another, be inclusive, and maybe give out some reparations here and there; and most of the world's problems will be solved.

While there are some good things that the social justice movement has done in history, the modern social movements are making things worse for the very people who they seek to liberate.

The feminist movement claims that women have less rights than men due to women earning less than men, not having instant access to all abortion measures, and getting less high-ranking positions than men, among other things.

The BLM movement claims that black people on average are more likely to be shot by a police officer or be a victim of racial profiling.

The fat acceptance movement claims that they are ostracized by society because they literally cannot fit in public spaces, and it is harder for them to get into relationships because they are not society's ideal body type.

The overarching thing that all of these movements claim is that they are all unfairly stereotyped and discriminated against and that action needs to be taken to fix these issues.

There are valid points that these movements are making as discrimination happens every day in some way, shape, or form, but the changes that the movements are championing are confusing at times. What people often fail to realize is that the action that is currently being taken ends up either discriminating against other groups or the action is detrimental to themselves.

The feminist movement has come to the point where corporations have almost been forced to hire more women than men, even if a man would be more suitable for the job. The NBA has to pay money out of their own pockets to keep the WNBA afloat. Feminism has gotten so out of hand that some men identify as female to gain the benefits that women have, which ends up hurting women even more, especially when it comes to female sports and privacy in bathrooms.

The BLM movement seeks to make other races pay for the injustice done to them in the days of slavery, but they fail to realize that most of the people who owned slaves have long since passed away. So, the ones that would be paying the price have nothing to do with the oppression that happened to them. Affirmative action that is often in collegiate universities often hurts the Asian communities as colleges are focusing more on diversity instead of accepting the smartest students.

The fat acceptance movement seeks to get others to adapt and pay for the life choices that they have made, others that also have no relation to the struggles that obesity can cause. Hospital beds need to be made larger to account for more people that weigh over 500 pounds, more drugs need to be given to treat the diseases that obesity often causes, and then everyone's healthcare costs go up to account for these extra expenditures.

Many problems that people want the government to fix can be fixed by following godly principles instead. Looking at the economy that God set forth for Israel in the Old Testament (dating from Moses's time to the days of the kings in Israel), we see that God naturally designed ways for people to harmoniously live together. We see clear and easy to follow laws that range from taking care of the poor and the widowed, forgiving debts after seven years of labor, and enforcing the laws while allowing room for discrepancies. Whether a citizen, servant, or stranger, everyone is held to the same moral standard. While we now follow the laws of America, we should still apply the same principles that God set in stone.

As stated earlier in Chapters 2-4, Christians can help those by donating their time or energy to charity.

Solomon is white and Isaiah is black, but we are tied together by our Christian faith and our similar viewpoints on society. While we can enjoy a sports game or a bagel together, our outlook on the world is what brings us to a more meaningful friendship. In western society, we often see "diversity for the sake of diversity" in schools, politics, and everyday life. We have seen and heard that all the time, and we would like to offer something different. No matter the person, the truth remains the same. Of course, it is nice having people who think the same but look different, or people who look the same but think differently. But at the end of the day, the truth is the same regardless of who you are or what background you have. People should be less concerned about how to diversify one's community and should be more focused on seeking the truth. When people do that, diversity happens on its own.

Truth brings people together by setting a standard that everyone can apply. Just like the residents of a country need to have something that ties them together from a patriotic standpoint, Christians need to come together under the truth of God, and everything else is secondary. Here is my example.

First, Christians need to be tied under the fact that Jesus is the Son of God and there is no other way to heaven except through Him. Next, Christians need to believe that the Bible is God's Word. Now I know that there are different translations and versions of the Bible, but at the very least Christians should believe in the core concepts of the Bible. This may be controversial, but I think that creationism and evolution should be a secondary argument (although it is an argument worth having) and not something that divides a church. On the other hand, things such as sexual sin should be a value that Christians should stand strong on and not budge if people want the church to be more lenient on things. Obviously, it is hard to follow God's Word 24/7, but that should be our goal as believers in Christ. For example, if someone in the church sins but is repentant, then everything is good. On the other side, if someone in the church sins but tries to justify their actions, then that is when the church should come and intervene.

An example of diversity gone bad is businesses that claim to promote diversity but are disingenuous. We see this clearly when companies post a black square during "black history month" or rainbow colors during "pride month," when in reality they are only doing it for marketing purposes. We know this because during pride month, the Middle Eastern logos remain the same Islam is not very fond of LGBTQ+ and companies do not want to lose their audiences by promoting ideals that the locals despise.

Diversity only works when there is at least one thing to unify everyone. For example, coworkers who work well together have the shared goal of helping the company grow. Family members each have different personalities, and although family members can step on each other's toes from time to time, the goal of having a safe, loving, and thriving family is normally enough for people to set aside their differences and walk in unity. Different branches in the military have different roles in the Air Force, Army, Marines, Navy, Coast Guard, and the Space Force. From the dedicated soldiers who risk their lives on the front lines to the civilian engineers who produce the weapons and technology needed to get an edge on any adversaries, every branch has the shared goal of keeping the country safe. The Bible even talks about the concept of body parts working together as one. 1 Corinthians 12:18-19 says, "But now God has set the members, each one of them, in the body just as He pleased. And if they were all one member, where would the body be?" (NKJV)

We need to all come together with our differences to push for truth in all avenues of life. We all have different gifts, different resources, and different people that we are able to interact with. Now is the time for us to come together as believers to preach to the end of the earth. That being said, it is good to talk about action, but it is another thing to actually follow the things that we say.

Words Are Cheap; Action Is Valuable

"BUT DON'T JUST LISTEN TO GOD'S WORD. YOU MUST DO WHAT IT SAYS. OTHERWISE, YOU ARE ONLY FOOLING YOURSELVES." JAMES 1:22 (NLT)

Peter swore to Jesus that he would stay by His side no matter what and even sliced off a soldier's ear to prove to Jesus that he would die for Him. But, as we all know, Peter later denied knowing Christ three times before sunrise. It can be easy to stand up for righteousness when others are in agreement with you, but it is obviously much more difficult when you are on an island. That is one of the reasons why a strong community is so important; it strengthens everyone inside the community to hold fast to their moral values and convictions.

Looking at China's underground church, when they say that they believe in Jesus, they really mean it as they are willing to lose their life for Him. The time will come when Christianity is frowned upon in America as well. Now is the time to strengthen our walks with God so that when we face persecution, we will not fold.

The parable of "separating the wheat from the tares" is something that we are beginning to see in modern society. Christianity is an interesting religion, from it being the most widespread religion in some countries, to being banned in others, and overall being the most widespread religion in the world. When given an award, you see big name celebrities and sports figures thank Jesus for giving them their talents. But when you look at some of their lives, it is hard to tell whether they truly love Jesus and if they actually are walking in God's ways. Obviously, we don't know their full relationship with God (that is between them and God), but we can observe their actions. In the present day it is easier and easier to judge someone by their "fruit," not their words. And it will only get more and more clear to determine which celebrities will continue to stand for God as Hollywood is evermore turning further away from God.

Christian lip-service does not contribute to the Christian faith because it does not produce any fruit that Christians should be bearing. We as Christians should make sure that our light is bright in times of trouble and times of relaxation.

COVID-19 was an example of how Christians as a whole were not strong in holding up their principles. Many communities closed down for far too long, with some communities still requiring masks and six feet distance. We Christians should have been promoting our faith in a dire situation.

Christians should have genuineness and consistency. If Christians don't strive to have a righteous representation, then it is questionable for you to claim that you are a Christian. Being a Christian should reflect every aspect of your life.

We need to be careful and examine ourselves and really ask the questions, am I a Christian? Can others tell that I am a Christian? What am I doing to walk righteously before God? The Bible says to remove the log from your own eye before removing the speck from someone else's eye.

Jesus is not fire insurance, and grace is not toilet paper. We should not accept Jesus and then go rogue and live the life the way we want. It is not the idea (or even the act) of accepting God: it is the authenticity of accepting Jesus into your heart. If someone is truly genuine about wanting to accept God into their hearts., then they will do everything in their power to follow His ways. Romans 6:1-2 says, "What shall we say then? Shall we continue in sin that grace may abound? Certainly not! How shall we who died to sin live any longer in it?" (NKJV) That verse means that because Jesus died for our sins, we should not continually wallow in and promote immoral behaviors.

We are not necessarily saying that Christians will always be perfect humans, but born again Christians have the ability to not sin because they are a new creature and are filled with the Holy Spirit. We should be aiming for perfection; even if we slip up we should pick ourselves up and get back on walking the straight and narrow path that God has called us to walk on. If you are a strong fruit-bearing Christian, it is not rocket science to preach God's Word. You don't have to be a deep theologian or a strong orator to be an effective witness. Because we truly believe in God, it should not be difficult for us to share how good God is.

We are by no means saying that Christians will never encounter doubt, fear, or uncertainty (quite the opposite actually), but we need to make sure that those things do not cripple us and stop us from doing what is right. In the story of Sodom and Gomorrah, angels told Lot and his family to flee from those wicked cities and to never look back. Unfortunately for Lot's wife, she looked back and was turned into a pillar of salt. While that is an extreme case of a consequence that happened to someone who did not listen to God, it is a sobering reminder that when we focus on the things of the world, we will get ourselves into trouble. When you experience doubt, stress, and anxiety, then it shows that you need God to help you on your walk. Doubt shows that you cannot do life on your own and that you need God to lead you.

If We Do Not Act, the World Will Cease to Exist

"BUT UNDERSTAND THIS, THAT IN THE LAST DAYS THERE WILL COME TIMES OF DIFFICULTY. FOR PEOPLE WILL BE LOVERS OF SELF, LOVERS OF MONEY, PROUD, ARROGANT, ABUSIVE, DISOBEDIENT TO THEIR PARENTS, UNGRATEFUL, UNHOLY, HEARTLESS, UNAPPEASABLE, SLANDEROUS, WITHOUT SELF-CONTROL, BRUTAL, NOT LOVING GOOD, TREACHEROUS, RECKLESS, SWOLLEN WITH CONCEIT, LOVERS OF PLEASURE RATHER THAN LOVERS OF GOD, HAVING THE APPEARANCE OF GODLINESS, BUT DENYING ITS POWER. AVOID SUCH PEOPLE."
2 TIMOTHY 3:1-5 (ESV)

Modern western society makes it easy for anyone to be a social recluse and have the luxury to be by oneself.

As a society, Christianity is declining all across the world, and we see Satanism on the rise. The main emphasis of society is currently to love yourself over anything else, and that is continuing to exacerbate itself as the days go by. The Doomsday clock is closer to midnight than ever before, and there is nothing reliable for people to put their hope and faith in. Morality becomes subjective or legalistic at best, and people tend to go to people deemed "superior" or "elite" to gain some type of direction in their lives. Can you imagine what America would be like if there were not any Christians in government, medicine, or science? We are already seeing it now. Late-term abortion and infanticide could be commonplace with Senate Bill 669 currently on the table that would allow for babies to be killed up to 28 days after they are born. Degeneracy and abnormal fetishes are currently mainstream, and in the near future I would not be surprised if heterosexual marriages become the minority. Sodom and Gomorrah in the United States is getting closer and closer, and it would be here now if it weren't for the Christians that are standing up for their beliefs. Crime is more rampant where there is no objective morality, and justice will not be fair and equitable for the victims of said crimes. Charity would almost cease to exist, the charity that is left will be filled with ulterior motives. The Hippocratic oath is a Christian concept; without it, science will turn into freak experiments and abominable acts of "research," similar to practices in concentration camps and Frankenstein-like experimentations.

All good things have Christian ties to them, unbeknownst to the world. That is why we must claim the good and reject the evil; there is no room for middle ground. It is a dog-eat-dog world out there, but we believers are above that. Our Holiness unto God will help us be a strong witness to others.

As Christians, we know that the world is doomed for eternity, but we are still called to bring heaven on earth. It is a fascinating dichotomy, as the worse the world gets the closer Jesus comes back to return.

Christians movements are a stopgap to the end; they allow a revitalization of godly principles to the masses. That is why we are promoting the gold standard.

The book of Esther is such a great example of believers in God stepping up in times in trouble. For those who need a refresher, during the Persian empire long ago, there was a man named Haman who wished to kill all the Jews. Due to surprising circumstances, a Jewish girl named Esther became queen of Persia. Esther had a choice whether to speak up for the Jews and risk her life, or to try and keep her Jewish heritage a secret for the rest of her life.

The pivotal point in the book is in chapter four when Mordecai kind of gives an ultimatum to Esther:

> *"And Mordecai told them to answer Esther: 'Do not think in your heart that you will escape in the king's palace any more than all the other Jews. For if you remain completely silent at this time, relief and deliverance will arise for the Jews from another place, but you and your father's house will perish. Yet who knows whether you have come to the kingdom for such a time as this?'" Esther 4:13-14 (NKJV)*

Esther stepped up to the plate and was able to stand up for her people through her acts of bravery and was able to kill Haman and the opposition that tried to eradicate the Jewish lineage. It is such a wonderful story that there is a yearly celebration of Esther's bravery called Purim.

God's plans will come to be, regardless of whether we want to follow Him or not. Jesus even said in Luke 19:40 that if the disciples did not openly proclaim God's goodness, the rocks would cry out.

> *"But He answered and said to them, 'I tell you that if these should keep silent, the stones would immediately cry out.'" Luke 19:40 (NKJV)*

If we do not stand up and spread the Good News of Christ, then God will call up someone else to do so. God's plans will happen whether we choose to follow Him or not, so what is the point of shying away from the spotlight?

Let's get back to Sodom and Gomorrah before it was destroyed. God sent angels to inform Abraham about how wicked the cities were and how they would soon be destroyed.

> *"Then the men turned away from there and went toward Sodom, but Abraham still stood before the Lord. And Abraham came near and said, 'Would You also destroy the righteous with the wicked? Suppose there were fifty righteous within the city; would You also destroy the place and not spare it for the fifty righteous that were in it? Far be it from You to do such a thing as this, to slay the righteous with the wicked, so that the righteous should be as the wicked; far be it from You! Shall not the Judge of all the earth do right?' So the Lord said, 'If I find in Sodom fifty righteous within the city, then I will spare all the place for their sakes.'" Genesis 18:22-26 (NKJV)*

Abraham then asks God if he would spare Sodom from destruction if there were 45 righteous men in the city, and God promises to spare the city from destruction as well. Then Abraham goes to 40, 35, 30, and eventually asks God if he would spare Sodom if there were ten righteous people in the city. God says yes, every time. Unfortunately for Sodom and Gomorrah, there weren't even ten righteous people living there, so God set the cities aflame.

I think that we are getting to a point in society where the western culture is a modern-day Sodom and Gomorrah. Crime and drugs run rampant in major cities, promiscuity is at an all-time high, and the only widespread taboo behaviors left are pedophilia and bestiality, and who knows how long it will be until those things are normalized.

Christians should not need to wait for a firecracker; we should be inspired on our own. We should not be overcome by evil but overcome evil with good. We can't stay in our basement bunkers and let the world rapidly descend into turmoil.

It is easy to be hypnotized by the pleasures of the world. And that is on purpose. You cannot go far without seeing advertisements for fashion, a new TV show, fast food, and luxury vacations. Media is designed to hook people and get them invested in things. Oftentimes, those things do not mean much of anything. As much as Isaiah loves the Miami Dolphins, even if they lose, he should not spiral into a hole of depression. Even if they win, while that is awesome, it does not change much in the spiritual realm. We should use entertainment to point others to values that represent Christ.

Video games, movies, and social media entertainment are fun, but we need to make sure that those things are not stopping us from interacting with others and witnessing to them.

An example of using entertainment for good is when playing basketball, you get to meet new people and eventually become acquaintances if you hang around for long enough, and if you carry yourself on the court relatively well. Similar to the workplace environment, if you hang around with people long enough, opportunities to converse happen. A simple question such as "how is your job going?" or "is the family okay?" can lead to long conversations, and people are usually more amenable to you talking about biblical things once you have already engaged in conversation.

Other examples of using entertainment for good are inviting people to watch the Super Bowl, playing online video games with friends, and going to amusement parks. Obviously, we need to be mindful about how much we partake in entertainment, but I venture to say that the issue is more regarding the fact that most people entertain themselves on their own. I am not saying that people should not go out to eat on their own, play single player games, or watch baseball highlights by themselves, as everyone needs time to relax. Isaiah himself can be very introverted at times. The problem is when we are so engrossed in our personal pastimes, we lose the opportunities to witness to others, and in turn we could be missing out on meaningful relationships. Isolation can eventually lead to depression, and depression tends to keep people from reaching out to others, further perpetuating a dangerous cycle. People often know some of the reasons why they are feeling down, but not everyone takes action to either seek help or to have a more fulfilling life.

Christians cannot have a doom and gloom mindset as we are less effective witnesses when we are sad. Nowadays it is seemingly normal for people to be depressed, and many of the causes why people are depressed range from abuse, medical conditions, and hormonal imbalances, but there are more people that are depressed because they have self-esteem issues, a pressure to grow up and handle more responsibilities, job unhappiness, the ongoing ups and downs in the economy, and no longer being able to easily communicate and connect with others in a relational way. If we are walking with God and following the Gold Standard of excellence, it will be harder for depression to tighten its hold on us.

The society that we live in gets its validation from whatever trends are on the rise, but Christians should get their validation from God. Walking in biblical truths and Judaic values gives us knowledge and wisdom that can be applied to the world. If we did not have the Good News to share with the world, then those who wish to escape the world will be left with nothing but bad news. Some people watch secular movies and listen to unwholesome music because they had no idea that Christian movies and music existed.

It is easy to hide ourselves from the world and worship God in secret, but we believe that God has called us to live unashamedly so we can be a light in the world. Even the Amish boldly live their lives without most modern technology but do it in a way that causes others to be inspired by their everyday life. What excuse do we have to not share the good news of Christ in our everyday lives? As people who are actively involved in social media and in the public square, we have every opportunity to be on the forefront of being effective witnesses. We need to do this for our families, our American values, and ultimately for our freedom.

For God, For Country, For Liberty

"YOU ARE THE LIGHT OF THE WORLD. A CITY SET ON A HILL CANNOT BE HIDDEN. NEITHER DO PEOPLE LIGHT A LAMP AND PUT IT UNDER A BASKET. INSTEAD, THEY PUT IT ON A LAMPSTAND SO IT GIVES LIGHT TO ALL IN THE HOUSE. IN THE SAME WAY, LET YOUR LIGHT SHINE BEFORE MEN SO THEY MAY SEE YOUR GOOD WORKS AND GLORIFY YOUR FATHER IN HEAVEN." MATTHEW 5:14-16 (TLV)

Every culture has a counterculture; we need to stand firm against the lies that the world spews. That involves working hard instead of being complacent, valuing others and not solely yourself, and loving others even when you have every right to hate them.

We want to stress the fact that true love and true justice go hand in hand; that is why a loving God can send people to hell.

We can love others and still not approve or validate an evil lifestyle; we need to use wisdom and discernment when confronting wickedness.

In my humble opinion, I think that Christians can either be hot or cold when it comes to integrating themselves in society, meaning that we should either jump headfirst and integrate ourselves in our communities, or be like nuns and monks, or even the Amish and separate from society.

Now, I think that Christians should first seek to get involved in their communities and spread the gospel through relationships and natural interactions, and God forbid if society rejects Christians, we will be able to start our own self-sustaining communities. Christians should learn things such as plumbing, electrical, medicinal, nutritional, biological, and agricultural occupations so that we can survive on our own.

Once again, this book is not intended to frighten believers and spread a doomsday message, but it is meant to empower Christians to live their best lives unto God. For those who are unbelievers but are on the fence, this is a call for us to turn to the only One who can give us true fulfillment in life. And just like Shadrach, Meshach, and Abednego in the fiery furnace, we shall trust in God, whether He saves us now or later. If you truly trust in God, there should be a peace that passes all understanding (Philippians 4:7) that will help you get through the different trials of life.

Being a Christian means that you should get some flak from the world, but we should be encouraged that we are fighting the good fight in the cultural and spiritual wars.

Being a Christian involves a significant amount of risks and potential hazards that impact both personal and professional aspects of one's life. This book highlights some of the most pressing occupational hazards of being a Christian.

Discrimination is one of the most significant occupational hazards of being a Christian. Christian workers may face discrimination in the workplace when it comes to rights, benefits, or promotions. This discrimination may be subtle or overt. In some cases, coworkers may isolate or marginalize an individual, making it difficult for them to work effectively.

Such discrimination may arise from differences in beliefs, practices, and values that are common among Christians. Additionally, Christian workers may face discrimination for taking a stand on social and moral issues, including those related to abortion, same-sex marriage, and gender identity.

Persecution, harassment, or violence against Christians is a worldwide problem that affects many countries, both in the west and in developing nations. Four of the top ten countries in the world where Christians face persecution are located in Sub-Saharan Africa.

In countries where Christians are the minority, violence and persecution can be particularly prevalent. Christians may face harassment, violence, or even death simply for practicing their faith. Extreme groups such as Boko Haram, Hezbollah, or the Islamic State would target Christians deliberately and kill them.

Many Christians are also the victims of violence due to affiliations, including those related to denominations or religious groups. While Christians, like any other individual, have a right to hold their beliefs, it is essential to be aware of physical safety in some areas.

The difficulty of finding employment is another significant occupational hazard for Christians. Many employers may discriminate against Christian job seekers, especially if they know about their religious background.

Employers may discriminate against them for various reasons, such as the belief that Christians are not fit for certain job functions or roles. These beliefs are usually accompanied by stereotypes that may not reflect the abilities and talents of the individual.

Being a Christian in modern times can be socially isolating because of the values and practices that often accompany it. It is not uncommon for Christians to face discrimination or stigma, both of which lead to isolation from friends and family members.

Stigmatization can lead to negative views and judgmental opinions from others, which can be distressing and harmful to Christian workers. Additionally, Christians may face social isolation because of their beliefs, which can impact their mental health and well-being.

It can also be challenging to find suitable business partners, organizations, or sponsors for the Christian worker's traditional value-based businesses, making it difficult to compete in the open market.

Evangelism involves sharing the Christian faith with others. While it is an essential part of Christian beliefs, it can be a hazardous activity. Evangelism may lead to confrontations, misunderstandings, or even conflict with others.

Christian workers who engage in evangelism may face consequences, including social isolation, discrimination, and legal issues. Additionally, evangelism may lead to misunderstandings and instances of cultural appropriation.

In some countries, evangelism is illegal or limited by law. These legal limitations may not arise due to discrimination; governments may also feel that such actions could lead to problems in society, e.g., riots or social unrest.

Being a Christian comes with several occupational hazards that can impact one's personal and professional life. Discrimination in the workplace, persecution and violence, the difficulty of finding employment, social isolation and stigmatization, and the consequences of evangelism are some of the most significant risks.

While some of these hazards cannot be avoided entirely, Christian workers can minimize their impact by being knowledgeable about their rights, seeking legal support when necessary, and adhering to cultural norms and values. Such hazards should not discourage a Christian from following their faith, as their belief can provide strength, guidance, and hope through difficult times.

The world's perspective of the gold standard and success has evolved over time. The idea of what success means varies between individuals, cultures, and societies. It is commonly equated with wealth, power, and status. The gold standard has been used in a variety of contexts to describe the pinnacle of achievement, be it economically, academically, or socially. In this essay, we will examine the different ways in which the world defines success and the gold standard.

One of the most commonly acknowledged ways of achieving success is through financial wealth. In today's globalized world, the accumulation of money and assets is often equated with success. The more successful someone is, the more money they earn or have. This idea of success is reinforced by the media and popular culture, which often portrays millionaires and billionaires as the ultimate goal. People admire those who have worked hard and have been able to achieve great wealth, often looking up to them and using them as role models.

Furthermore, success can manifest in the form of power and status. People who hold positions of authority, such as politicians, business executives, and celebrities, are perceived as successful. They are regarded as people who have worked hard and have been able to achieve high positions in society. This type of success often brings with it the power and influence to make decisions that have far-reaching consequences.

In the field of academia, success is measured by a person's level of education and their contributions to the academic community. Achieving a Ph.D. or a doctorate in a specialized field can be seen as the gold standard of success. Academics who publish their research in well-regarded academic journals are also viewed as successful, and their work can have a lasting impact on their field of study.

Another facet of success is personal fulfillment and happiness. While financial wealth, power, and status are often the most accepted forms of success, they do not necessarily lead to satisfaction and happiness. Many individuals seek success in their personal relationships, hobbies, and passions. For some, success means being able to pursue their passions and being content with their daily lives. For others, success means having a healthy work/life balance and being able to spend time with their family and friends.

In conclusion, the world's idea of the gold standard and success has evolved over time. While financial wealth, power, and status are often the most commonly accepted forms of success, people are still striving for more meaningful achievements such as personal fulfillment and happiness. It is important to recognize that success can take many forms, and what works for one person may not work for another. Ultimately, the pursuit of success is a personal journey, and individuals must determine what success means to them and what they are willing to sacrifice to achieve it.

Christianity has had a profound impact on the world for over 2,000 years. The faith has inspired some of the most influential thinkers and leaders the world has ever known, from St. Augustine to Martin Luther King Jr. The contributions of Christian champions to society are innumerable, from scientific discoveries to social justice movements. However, the question of what the world would look like without Christian champions is an intriguing one. While it is impossible to know for certain, it is worthwhile to explore the possibilities.

One of the most significant contributions that Christianity has made to the world is in the field of science and medicine. Christian champions such as Saint Albertus Magnus, who was one of the first naturalists, laid the foundation for modern science. Additionally, the early contributions of Christian scientists like Johannes Kepler, who discovered the laws of planetary motion, and Sir Isaac Newton, who formulated the laws of gravity, laid the foundation for our modern understanding of the world.

Through the influence of Christian champions on the development of modern science, the world has seen tremendous advancements in medicine, specifically. Christian medical missionaries have had a significant impact on the health and well-being of people in developing countries. Christian doctors and nurses around the world continue to save lives through their work in medicine, and it is difficult to imagine what the world would be like without their contributions.

Christianity has also had a profound impact on art and culture around the world. From architecture to painting, music to literature, Christian champions have inspired some of the most beautiful and enduring works of art. The works of Michelangelo, Bach, and C.S. Lewis, among many others, have shaped the way we think about beauty, truth, and goodness.

Without Christian champions, the world would be poorer for the absence of these works of art. Additionally, the role of Christianity in shaping our understanding of beauty and truth cannot be overstated. Christian champions throughout history have given us a language for articulating the significance of beauty and truth in our lives. If we were to remove these contributions from our understanding of art and culture, the world would be more bleak and less inspiring.

Perhaps one of the most significant contributions of Christian champions has been to social justice movements. Throughout history, Christians have been at the forefront of movements for civil rights, abolition, and the protection of the vulnerable. Without Christian champions, it is difficult to imagine how these movements would have been successful.

The work of Christian champions like William Wilberforce, who fought tirelessly against the slave trade, and Martin Luther King Jr., who led the fight for civil rights in America, have shaped the course of history. The contributions of Christian champions to social justice are ongoing, as Christians continue to work for the protection of the unborn, the fight against human trafficking, and the fight against poverty around the world.

It is impossible to know exactly what the world would look like without Christian champions. However, one can speculate that without the contributions of these champions, the world would be a much different place. Science, medicine, art, and social justice would all be different if Christianity had not influenced them. It is clear that the contributions of Christian champions have been profound and ongoing, and we should be grateful for their influence on the world.

As believers in Christ, Christians have a mandate to participate actively in the public sphere and to help bring about change in government and other societal institutions. Here are some practical ways in which Christians can make a difference:

- Christians can make a significant impact on government and other societal institutions by praying for them. Prayer is a powerful tool that can transform hearts, minds, and situations that appear hopeless. As Christians, we are called to pray for those in leadership positions, that they may be guided by wisdom and discernment to make decisions that promote the common good. We can also pray for other societal institutions, such as the education system, media, and justice system, that they may be transformed by the power of God.

- Churches and Christian organizations can play a significant role in shaping government policies and promoting the values of morality, truth, justice, and compassion. Christians can actively participate in politics by voting for candidates who share their values, running for office themselves, or supporting advocacy groups that lobby for change. Through their involvement in the political process, Christians can help shape policies that promote the common good, defend human rights, and advance the interests of the marginalized.

- Christians can promote transparency and accountability in government and other societal institutions by demanding transparency and accountability from leaders and institutions. This can be done through social accountability mechanisms, such as public participation, citizen watchdog groups, and public interest litigation. Christians can also advocate for laws that promote transparency and accountability, such as freedom of information laws and whistleblower protection laws.

- Corruption is a significant challenge facing governments worldwide. It undermines the rule of law, damages the economy, and perpetuates poverty. Christians can make a difference by fighting corruption in all its forms, whether it is through bribery, nepotism, or embezzlement of public funds. This can be done through various means, such as reporting corrupt practices, advocating for anti-corruption policies, and promoting ethical leadership.

- Justice is a core value of Christianity, and Christians are called to seek justice for all. Christians can make a difference by advancing the cause of justice in society, whether it is through fighting discrimination, advocating for the rights of the vulnerable, or supporting the rule of law. Christians can also support organizations that provide legal assistance to the marginalized, such as victims of human trafficking, refugees, and asylum seekers.

- Finally, Christians can make a difference by promoting healthy families, which are the foundation of society. Healthy families provide a nurturing environment for children to grow and develop into responsible adults who can contribute to society positively. Christians can promote healthy families by supporting pro-family policies, providing counseling and support services to families, and advocating for family-friendly working conditions.

The modern American Christian church has seen significant deterioration over the years, with certain trends impacting its relevance, influence, and ability to carry out its mission. From the increasing focus on entertainment to the lack of spiritual depth, several factors have contributed to this decline.

First, the modern American Christian church has become more focused on entertainment than on spiritual growth. Many churches have turned to using music, videos, and other forms of visual stimulation to attract more members. While this may help raise attendance in the short term, it ultimately fails to create a lasting connection between members and God. By relying on entertainment rather than spiritual depth, churches risk fostering superficial faith that is ill-equipped to grapple with life's challenges.

Second, the modern American church has become more individualistic than communal. Many churches have shifted from being a community center to a "personal enhancement center." Members are no longer expected to take part in the communal life of the church but rather to consume it as a product. This shift has led to a lack of intimacy, accountability, and vulnerability, which are necessary for authentic Christian growth. As a result, many modern churches are more like corporations, and members are treated like customers rather than brothers and sisters in Christ.

Third, the modern American Christian church has become more politically polarized. As the country has become increasingly divided along political lines, so has the church. Many churches have taken sides on political issues and become battlegrounds for political campaigning rather than sanctuaries of God's grace. This has led to a sense of alienation among members who do not share the same political views and has hurt the church's ability to witness to the world.

Additionally, the church has failed to challenge members to think critically about their faith. Instead of encouraging members to explore and question their beliefs, many churches have adopted a "party line" mentality that encourages conformity over engagement. This reluctance to address complex issues and engage with doubts and questions has led to a lack of intellectual curiosity and a superficial understanding of faith.

Furthermore, the church has become more consumer-driven at the expense of service. Many members view church as a place to consume programs and resources rather than engaging with the world in service. This view of the church contradicts the Gospel message of a call to service and mission, resulting in a lack of engagement with pressing social issues and the mission of the church.

In conclusion, the modern American Christian church has experienced significant deterioration over the years due to entertainment-driven, individualistic, politically polarized, and consumer-oriented trends. These trends have impoverished the church's ability to nourish deep, long-lasting faith, undermined its community-building capacity, and distracted it from its mission of service and witness to the world. If the church hopes to regain its relevance and influence, it must reform its practices and prioritize spiritual depth, community, service, and critical thought.

Christian and American Exceptionalism

Christianity and American culture are inextricably linked, and this has led to the idea of Christian exceptionalism and American exceptionalism. Christian exceptionalism is the idea that Christianity is superior to other religions and that Christians have a special role to play in the world. American exceptionalism, on the other hand, is the idea that the United States of America is a unique and exceptional nation with a special destiny to spread democracy and freedom throughout the world. In this essay, I will argue that Christian exceptionalism and American exceptionalism go hand in hand and are rooted in the same cultural and historical traditions.

One of the main reasons why Christian exceptionalism and American exceptionalism are closely linked is because Christianity has played a central role in American history and culture from the very beginning. The Pilgrims, who founded the Plymouth Colony in 1620, were devout Christians who believed that they had been chosen by God to create a new society based on Christian principles. Similarly, the Founding Fathers, who wrote the Declaration of Independence and the Constitution, were deeply influenced by Christian ideas of morality and justice. Many of them were also members of Christian denominations, and they saw the United States as a new Israel, a chosen people with a special mission to spread liberty and democratic values throughout the world.

This idea of America as a "city on a hill" or a beacon of hope for the world has been a recurring theme in American political and cultural discourse. It is often accompanied by religious rhetoric and appeals to Christian values. For example, in his famous speech to the United Nations in 1982, President Ronald Reagan invoked the idea of American exceptionalism and the need to defend freedom and democracy against the forces of tyranny and oppression. In Reagan's farewell speech, he also used explicitly Christian language and referenced Matthew 5:14, saying that "America is a shining city upon a hill whose beacon light guides freedom-loving people everywhere."

Another reason why Christian exceptionalism and American exceptionalism are closely linked is because they both reflect a deep sense of optimism and idealism about the future. Christians believe that God has a plan for the world and that history is moving toward an ultimate goal of redemption and salvation. Similarly, Americans believe that their country has a special destiny to lead the world toward a better future and that through hard work, innovation, and democratic values, the United States can create a prosperous and just society for all.

This sense of optimism and idealism has often been expressed in terms of exceptionalism, the idea that America and Christianity have a unique role to play in the world. This can sometimes lead to arrogance and ethnocentrism as Americans and Christians may believe that their way of life is better than others and that they have a right to impose their values on other cultures. However, it can also lead to a sense of responsibility and a desire to make the world a better place as Americans and Christians feel a deep sense of obligation to use their power and influence for the common good.

Finally, Christian exceptionalism and American exceptionalism are closely linked because they share common enemies and challenges. Both Christians and Americans have faced opposition and persecution from outside forces, whether it be the Roman Empire, the British Empire, or the Soviet Union. Both have also faced internal challenges, such as moral decay and social fragmentation, that threaten to undermine their values and way of life.

In response to these challenges, Christians and Americans have often found strength and inspiration in their exceptionalism, the idea that they are a chosen people with a special destiny. This exceptionalism has helped them to overcome adversity and to stay true to their principles, even in the face of overwhelming opposition.

Christian exceptionalism and American exceptionalism are closely linked and reflect a deep sense of optimism and idealism about the future. Both are rooted in the history and culture of the United States, and both reflect a sense of responsibility and obligation to use their power and influence for the common good. While this exceptionalism can sometimes lead to arrogance and ethnocentrism, it can also inspire individuals and nations to work toward a better world, grounded in Christian values of justice, compassion, and love.

This book has progressed, and the foundational elements of individual Christians projecting and living out the gold standard on a daily basis has been articulated. It is important to note that all of it means nothing if we as Christian believers across this country do not heed these words of wisdom and the warning signs of societal deterioration and reinvigorate our society with morality, truth, and ambition that is needed to bring this country out of the steep decline it is headed in. The time for action is now; not tomorrow or a month from now, and not when we feel comfortable as Christian believers. We must emphasize the importance of community outreach, boldly standing up against the evil that has begun to creep in toward institutions and ensure that we are flooding every societal area to ensure that we have Christians dominating in every aspect of our culture.

Currently, we are not in a physical battle for our country but rather a culture war. This culture war can only be won if we have strong Christian leaders and an "army" behind them to take on opponents that seek to establish legislation that completely contradicts the values that we as Christians hold dear. In addition, this culture war must be acknowledged by Christians, because if we do not recognize and identify who we are fighting against, we will never win.

From the halls of Congress to Yankee stadium fields to classrooms and church pews, this culture war must be fought by every single one of us. Our contribution and impact will be determined by a resolve and steadfast commitment to promoting and projecting Christian faith across all cultural battlefronts.

As you come to the conclusion of this book, don't just finish this chapter and put it on the bookshelf to collect dust and then begin a new novel. Use the inspirations and the truths that have been spoken and sound the alarms that the Christian church and believers across this nation need to rise up and take charge to preserve our very way of life. Actions speak louder than words. Rhetoric and sexy speeches will do nothing to achieve the Gold Standard that this book states. The Gold Standard can only be fulfilled when believers across the land get up, stand up, and are bold and courageous in their Christian faith. Christianity is a personal, individual relationship with God, not a collection of sentiments or a cool thing to identify as. Only those with enough conviction, confidence, and courage answer the call to arms in a country to take a stand against evil and go back to the times when Christians were in the public square championing the word of God and the worldview that stems from it.

At Liberty University, Isaiah and Solomon were taught that when it's all said and done, no matter what your major, your passions, or your hobbies, the main takeaway is the strive to be a Champion for Christ. This country needs more courageous champions for Christ that will stand up and not only spread the truth of Christ but boldly defend His word and those who value the flag and the values that the flag stands for. We have seen time and time again how successful we can be, not only as a nation but as a Christian faith on this earth when good leaders are in positions of power and influence. We need leaders to step up from this new generation and take on the challenge that every generation before them has answered: the call to preserve the foundational principles and freedoms of this nation and to ensure that Christianity and the principles and beliefs that ultimately flow from it are not removed from the public square, the classrooms of our schools, the higher grounds of our sports venues, the news anchor rooms, and the churches scattered all across this great land.

It is with great urgency that we say this. Our nation and quite frankly our entire world is at a tipping point. Do we, the people of the United States, return the principles and beliefs that made our country great and caused a majority of our society to thrive, or do we continue our path towards secularization in the promotion of values that are nowhere near what God would have intended for His creation? It is with this that we leave you with a rallying cry to invigorate you in the battles that you will encounter ahead. Our country does not worship governments but God and the rights, liberties, and privileges we enjoy every single day that ultimately stem from Him. When you close this book, keep it and the principles that I've been ingrained within you nearby as a reminder to keep up the good fight and not grow weary in doing good. Understand the challenges ahead and that this will not be an easy fight to win, but as Christians we have the confidence that we will be victorious.

So, for a person fresh out of high school or college who is just getting into the workforce, what steps should be taken? Some people know exactly what they want to do, but what if you are not sure about what your "calling" in life? What if you don't know whether you want to continue your education at an institution or start your own business or raise a family? Well, we believe that if you aren't sure what God is telling you to do, then the next step would be to pray, look at the various options that you have, and to just take different opportunities that come up. If you have free time to volunteer for an organization, work a couple shifts at a coffee shop, or do some yard work for a family member, then you should do those things. Even hanging out with friends and creating positive experiences is an easy way to follow the Gold Standard and be a light to others. As long as you are following the ways of God in your actions and your interactions, you probably can't go wrong in choosing whatever vocation(s) that you would like. If you feel like you have a clear calling from God to do a specific thing, then you would be able to pivot and continue your public walk with God.

Let's assume that you have already found "who you are as a person" and have a vision laid out for yourself.

1. Find a job and establish yourself in the workforce. If you cannot get a job in your field, then keep yourself busy while you wait. Similar to what was stated earlier, you can apply for entry-level jobs outside of your field to gain working experience, or you can spend quality time with friends and family while you apply for various jobs. Once you get hired

into the workforce, do your best to create camaraderie and become a trusted employee.

2. Find a vibrant Christian community and establish yourself there (especially if you plan on living there for at least a year). Find a community that will help you grow! You can do this by visiting local churches until you find a place where you can serve and worship and be held accountable as you develop your faith. If you cannot find any churches nearby, then you can look online for churches that you can integrate in, or you can start a church, Bible study, or worship night of your own! It is vital that you become friends with like-minded Christians that share your values and can encourage you.

3. Make intentional inroads of your faith consistently in the workplace (consistency can't be stressed enough!) With this step, you should be wise in how you spread the gospel at the workplace. Consistent excellency is the easiest form of being an effective witness. Obviously, mistakes will happen at work at some point in time, but when people see you striving to hold yourself to a higher standard, they will be appreciative of your efforts and are more likely to support you. You should also make sure that you are not boasting about your achievements but instead are doing your work humbly. When talking to others (especially in the workplace) you should not seek to distract others from their tasks by bombarding them with Bible Scriptures or spiritual debates, but instead your speech and conduct should be Christ-like. Saying small things such as, "Prayerfully this task goes smoothly" or "God bless you for helping me out today" can go a long way.

4. Lay out a path for future elevation in your vocation (be ambitious). Shoot for the stars and set some stretch goals, and also be realistic and set some small milestones. No dream is too big or too small! Whether you want to own your own business, feed the poor in every continent, or become president of the United States, you should plan to achieve those things. By laying out the steps required and getting information, you will be more equipped to excel, and you will be more focused on attaining your goals. A simple way to start is by creating new year's resolutions (no more than twelve) and trying to finish one goal per month. Once you can successfully conquer short-term goals, then you can branch out and create three-year, five-year, ten-year goals, and so forth and so on.

5. Perfect a balance between work, family, and faith. Being active in your job, your church, and your communities can become difficult at times. Your boss may want you to work overtime for an important project, your church may be hosting a Bible study from 7-9pm every Wednesday, and your family may want to go on a road trip for a couple of days. These events could be happening simultaneously or could be happening back-to-back-to-back. It is important that you prioritize your faith and family above any extra work events, but you should also make sure that you are not neglecting your work responsibilities either. A perfect work-life balance varies from person to person, so you must pray and use wisdom when discerning how to spend your time. You may not always have a perfect balance of these things, but if you make a conscious effort to do so, you should be able to reduce

burnout and stress.

Continual consistency of exceptional behavior of these 5 pillars will start the process of invigoration within oneself. Thank you for reading this book, and may God give you blessings, courage, and the ability to choose excellence and follow the Gold Standard.

Scriptural Index

"But know this, that in the last days perilous times will come: For men will be lovers of themselves, lovers of money, boasters, proud, blasphemers, disobedient to parents, unthankful, unholy, unloving, unforgiving, slanderers, without self-control, brutal, despisers of good, traitors, headstrong, haughty, lovers of pleasure rather than lovers of God, having a form of godliness but denying its power. And from such people turn away! For of this sort are those who creep into households and make captives of gullible women loaded down with sins, led away by various lusts, always learning and never able to come to the knowledge of the truth. Now as Jannes and Jambres resisted Moses, so do these also resist the truth: men of corrupt minds, disapproved concerning the faith; but they will progress no further, for their folly will be manifest to all, as theirs also was.

But you have carefully followed my doctrine, manner of life, purpose, faith, longsuffering, love, perseverance, persecutions, afflictions, which happened to me at Antioch, at Iconium, at Lystra—what persecutions I endured. And out of them all the Lord delivered me. Yes, and all who desire to live godly in Christ Jesus will suffer persecution. But evil men and impostors will grow worse and worse, deceiving and being deceived. But you must continue in the things which you have learned and been assured of, knowing from whom you have learned them, and that from childhood you have known the Holy Scriptures, which are able to make you wise for salvation through faith which is in Christ Jesus.

All Scripture is given by inspiration of God, and is profitable for doctrine, for reproof, for correction, for instruction in righteousness, that the man of God may be complete, thoroughly equipped for every good work.

2 Timothy 3 (NKJV)

And seeing the multitudes, He went up on a mountain, and when He was seated His disciples came to Him. Then He opened His mouth and taught them, saying:

"Blessed are the poor in spirit,

For theirs is the kingdom of heaven.

Blessed are those who mourn,

For they shall be comforted.

Blessed are the meek,

For they shall inherit the earth.

Blessed are those who hunger and thirst for righteousness,

For they shall be filled.

Blessed are the merciful,

For they shall obtain mercy.

Blessed are the pure in heart,

For they shall see God.

Blessed are the peacemakers,

For they shall be called sons of God.

Blessed are those who are persecuted for righteousness' sake,

For theirs is the kingdom of heaven.

Blessed are you when they revile and persecute you, and say all kinds of evil against you falsely for My sake. Rejoice and be exceedingly glad, for great is your reward in heaven, for so they persecuted the prophets who were before you."

"You are the salt of the earth; but if the salt loses its flavor, how shall it be seasoned? It is then good for nothing but to be thrown out and trampled underfoot by men.

You are the light of the world. A city that is set on a hill cannot be hidden. Nor do they light a lamp and put it under a basket, but on a lampstand, and it gives light to all who are in the house. Let your light so shine before men, that they may see your good works and glorify your Father in heaven."

"Do not think that I came to destroy the Law or the Prophets. I did not come to destroy but to fulfill. For assuredly, I say to you, till heaven and earth pass away, one jot or one tittle will by no means pass from the law till all is fulfilled. Whoever therefore breaks one of the least of these commandments, and teaches men so, shall be called least in the kingdom of heaven; but whoever does and teaches them, he shall be called great in the kingdom of heaven. For I say to you, that unless your righteousness exceeds the righteousness of the scribes and Pharisees, you will by no means enter the kingdom of heaven."

"You have heard that it was said to those of old, 'You shall not murder, and whoever murders will be in danger of the judgment.' But I say to you that whoever is angry with his brother without a cause shall be in danger of the judgment. And whoever says to his brother, 'Raca!' shall be in danger of the council. But whoever says, 'You fool!' shall be in danger of hell fire. Therefore if you bring your gift to the altar, and there remember that your brother has something against you, leave your gift there before the altar, and go your way. First be reconciled to your brother, and then come and offer your gift. Agree with your adversary quickly, while you are on the way with him, lest your adversary deliver you to the judge, the judge hand you over to the officer, and you be thrown

into prison. Assuredly, I say to you, you will by no means get out of there till you have paid the last penny."

"You have heard that it was said to those of old, 'You shall not commit adultery.' But I say to you that whoever looks at a woman to lust for her has already committed adultery with her in his heart. If your right eye causes you to sin, pluck it out and cast it from you; for it is more profitable for you that one of your members perish, than for your whole body to be cast into hell. And if your right hand causes you to sin, cut it off and cast it from you; for it is more profitable for you that one of your members perish, than for your whole body to be cast into hell."

"Furthermore it has been said, 'Whoever divorces his wife, let him give her a certificate of divorce.' But I say to you that whoever divorces his wife for any reason except sexual immorality causes her to commit adultery; and whoever marries a woman who is divorced commits adultery."

"Again you have heard that it was said to those of old, 'You shall not swear falsely, but shall perform your oaths to the Lord.' But I say to you, do not swear at all: neither by heaven, for it is God's throne; nor by the earth, for it is His footstool; nor by Jerusalem, for it is the city of the great King. Nor shall you swear by your head, because you cannot make one hair white or black. But let your 'Yes' be 'Yes,' and your 'No,' 'No.' For whatever is more than these is from the evil one."

"You have heard that it was said, 'An eye for an eye and a tooth for a tooth.' But I tell you not to resist an evil person. But whoever slaps you on your right cheek, turn the other to him also. If anyone wants to sue you and take away your tunic, let him have your cloak also. And whoever compels you to go one mile, go with him two. Give to him who asks you, and from him who wants to borrow from you do not turn away."

"You have heard that it was said, 'You shall love your neighbor and hate your enemy.' But I say to you, love your enemies, bless those who curse you, do good to those who hate you, and pray for those who spitefully use *you and persecute you, that you may be sons of your Father in heaven; for He makes His sun rise on the evil and on the good, and sends rain on the just and on the unjust. For if you love those who love you, what reward have you? Do not even the tax collectors do the same? And if you greet your brethren only, what do you do more than others? Do not even the tax collectors do so? Therefore you shall be perfect, just as your Father in heaven is perfect."*

Matthew 5 (NKJV)

"Servants, be submissive to your masters with all fear, not only to the good and gentle, but also to the harsh. For this is commendable, if because of conscience toward God one endures grief, suffering wrongfully. For what credit is it if, when you are beaten for your faults, you take it patiently? But when you do good and suffer, if you take it patiently, this is commendable before God. For to this you were called, because Christ also suffered for us, leaving us an example, that you should follow His steps: "Who committed no sin, Nor was deceit found in His mouth"; who, when He was reviled, did not revile in return; when He suffered, He did not threaten, but committed Himself to Him who judges righteously; who Himself bore our sins in His own body on the tree, that we, having died to sins, might live for righteousness— by whose stripes you were healed."

I Peter 2:18-24 (NKJV)

"For we are His workmanship, created in Christ Jesus for good works, which God prepared beforehand that we should walk in them."

Ephesians 2:10 (NKJV)

"If then you were raised with Christ, seek those things which are above, where Christ is, sitting at the right hand of God. Set your mind on things

above, not on things on the earth. For you died, and your life is hidden with Christ in God. When Christ who is our life appears, then you also will appear with Him in glory.

Therefore put to death your members which are on the earth: fornication, uncleanness, passion, evil desire, and covetousness, which is idolatry. Because of these things the wrath of God is coming upon the sons of disobedience, in which you yourselves once walked when you lived in them.

But now you yourselves are to put off all these: anger, wrath, malice, blasphemy, filthy language out of your mouth.Do not lie to one another, since you have put off the old man with his deeds, and have put on the new man who is renewed in knowledge according to the image of Him who created him, where there is neither Greek nor Jew, circumcised nor uncircumcised, barbarian, Scythian, slave nor free, but Christ is all and in all. Therefore, as the elect of God, holy and beloved, put on tender mercies, kindness, humility, meekness, longsuffering; bearing with one another, and forgiving one another, if anyone has a complaint against another; even as Christ forgave you, so you also must do. But above all these things put on love, which is the bond of perfection. And let the peace of God rule in your hearts, to which also you were called in one body; and be thankful. Let the word of Christ dwell in you richly in all wisdom, teaching and admonishing one another in psalms and hymns and spiritual songs, singing with grace in your hearts to the Lord. And whatever you do in word or deed, do all in the name of the Lord Jesus, giving thanks to God the Father through Him.

Wives, submit to your own husbands, as is fitting in the Lord.

Husbands, love your wives and do not be bitter toward them.

Children, obey your parents in all things, for this is well pleasing to the Lord.

Fathers, do not provoke your children, lest they become discouraged.

Bondservants, obey in all things your masters according to the flesh, not with eyeservice, as men-pleasers, but in sincerity of heart, fearing God. And whatever you do, do it heartily, as to the Lord and not to men, knowing that from the Lord you will receive the reward of the inheritance; for you serve the Lord Christ. But he who does wrong will be repaid for what he has done, and there is no partiality."
Colossians 3 (NKJV)

"And we know that all things work together for good to those who love God, to those who are the called according to His purpose."
Romans 8:28 (NKJV)

"But as for those whose hearts follow the desire for their detestable things and their abominations, I will recompense their deeds on their own heads," says the Lord GOD."
Ezekiel 11:21 (NKJV)

"Delight yourself also in the LORD, And He shall give you the desires of your heart."
Psalms 37:4 (NKJV)

"No temptation has overtaken you except such as is common to man; but God is faithful, who will not allow you to be tempted beyond what you are able, but with the temptation will also make the way of escape, that you may be able to bear it."
I Corinthians 10:13 (NKJV)

"Therefore submit to God. Resist the devil and he will flee from you."
James 4:7 (NKJV)

"Be sober, be vigilant; because your adversary the devil walks about like a roaring lion, seeking whom he may devour. Resist him, steadfast in the faith, knowing that the same sufferings are experienced by your brotherhood in the world."

I Peter 5:8-9 (NKJV)

"Blessed is the man who endures temptation; for when he has been approved, he will receive the crown of life which the Lord has promised to those who love Him. Let no one say when he is tempted, "I am tempted by God"; for God cannot be tempted by evil, nor does He Himself tempt anyone. But each one is tempted when he is drawn away by his own desires and enticed. Then, when desire has conceived, it gives birth to sin; and sin, when it is full-grown, brings forth death. Do not be deceived, my beloved brethren."

James 1:12-16 (NKJV)

"Dear friends, let us continue to love one another, for love comes from God. Anyone who loves is a child of God and knows God. 8 But anyone who does not love does not know God, for God is love."

1 John 4:7-8 (NLT)

"Always be humble and gentle. Be patient with each other, making allowance for each other's faults because of your love."

Ephesians 4:2 (NLT)

"My little children, let us not love in word or in tongue, but in deed and in truth."

I John 3:18 (NKJV)

"Love does no harm to a neighbor; therefore love is the fulfillment of the law."

Romans 13:10 (NKJV)

"Hatred stirs up strife, But love covers all sins."

Proverbs 10:12 (NKJV)

References

Chapter One:

The Declaration of Independence

Worldview, Saffron. *Know the 26 Controversial Verses of Quran Waseem Rizvi Wants Deleted.* Kreately, 2021.

Chapter Four:

Top 10 Marriage Failure Reasons. Divorce.com, 2023.

TakingtheRainbowBack.com

Mayberry, Carly. *U.K. Pastor Arrested After Anti-Same-Sex Marriage Comments Back on Stump With Politician's Support.* Newsweek, 2021.

Chapter Six:

Sanchez, Rosa. *Gisel Bündchen Breaks Her Silence on Why She and Tom Brady Split.* Bazaar, 2023.

Robinson, Sandra. *Is Tom Brady Religious?* Celeb Answers, 2021.

Colton, Graham. *Andrew Tate claims big tech banned him after 'large swaths' of people agreed with his 'masculine values.'* Fox News, 2022.

Sabes, Adam. *Andrew Tate Released From Romanian Jail, Placed Under House Arrest.* Fox News, 2023.

Stardom? I'd Rather Be An Insignificant Speck, Claims Keira. Evening Standard, 2007.

McKenzie, Joi-Marie. *Kristen Stewart Says 'Fame Is the Worst Thing in the World.'* ABC News, 2015.

Bate, Ellie. *Justin Bieber Has Given A Brutally Honest Interview About the Effects of Fame.* BuzzFeed, 2015.

Mary-Kate Olsen Breaks Her Silence. Marie Claire, 2010.

Weiss, Shari. *Billy Ray Cyrus in QC: My family is under attack by Satan, I'm 'scared for' daughter Miley.* Daily News, 2011.

Famous People Who Sold Their Souls to the Devil. Slapped Ham, 2019.

Wallin, Emily. *30 Famous Selena Gomez Quotes.* Wealthy Gorilla, 2023.

Badziag, Rafael. *I spent six years interviewing 21 billionaires. I found that the 1% are happier than the average person — and it's not just because they're rich.* Insider, 2019.

Wallace, Francesca. *Meghan Markle once admitted she dreamt of becoming a royal like "Princess Kate".* Vogue, 2018.

Chapter Nine:

Hamner, Suzanne. *Maryland Senate Bill 669 Legalizes Infanticide Up To 28 Days After Birth.* The Washington Standard, 2022.

Chapter Ten:

Ronald Reagan and "The Shining City Upon A Hill." Our Lost Founding, 2021.

Farewell Address to the Nation. ReaganFoundation.org